ALSO BY FRED BROCK

Live Well on Less Than You Think:
The New York Times Guide to Achieving Your Financial Freedom

Retire on Less Than You Think:
The New York Times Guide to Planning Your Financial Future

Health Care on Less Than You Think

Health Care
on Less
Than You Think

The New York Times
GUIDE TO GETTING
AFFORDABLE COVERAGE

FRED BROCK

TIMES BOOKS
HENRY HOLT AND COMPANY | NEW YORK

Times Books
Henry Holt and Company, LLC
Publishers since 1866
175 Fifth Avenue
New York, New York 10010

Henry Holt® is a registered trademark of
Henry Holt and Company, LLC.

Library of Congress Cataloging-in-Publication Data
Brock, Fred.
  Health care on less than you think : the New York Times guide to getting affordable
coverage/ Fred Brock.—1st ed.
    p. cm.
  Includes index.
  ISBN-13: 978-0-8050-7980-7
  ISBN-10: 0-8050-7980-7
  1. Medical care—United States—Finance.   2. Medical care, Cost of—United States.
3. Insurance, Health—United States.   4. Finance, Personal—United States.   I. New York
times.   II. Title
RA410.53.B754 2006
362.1068'1—dc22   2006045659

Henry Holt books are available for special promotions and
premiums. For details contact: Director, Special Markets.

First Edition 2006

Illustrations by Pat Lyons
Designed by Kelly Too

Printed in the United States of America
10 9 8 7 6 5 4 3 2 1

contents

Introduction: In the Waiting Room   ix

1. Spending More, Getting Less   1

2. Protect Your Health, Protect Your Budget   31

3. Off the Job   59

4. Health Savings Accounts   71

5. The State of Your Health and the State Where You Live   95

6. Rx for Your Wallet   119

7. Mastering Your Insurer's Fine Print   145

8. Planning for Medicare   159

9. The Threat to Your Savings and Retirement   177

10. Sorting Out Your Options   187

Afterword: A New Framework   201

Resources   209

Acknowledgments   214

Index   215

Introduction: In the Waiting Room

Waiting in a medical office to see a doctor not long ago, I couldn't help overhearing the conversation of a young couple seated across from me. He, wearing work clothes and mud-caked boots, looked worried; she was in tears. I picked up that he had some kind of kidney ailment and was trying to see a doctor. The couple had no health insurance, and the receptionist had told them that the doctor wouldn't treat the young man unless he first paid a $300 deposit. Apparently, some previous bills had not been paid. The two were discussing whether they should try to scrounge up the money or forgo treatment and hope he would get better. They finally left, after deciding to ask a relative for a loan. "I don't know what we'll do if you have to go to the hospital," the young woman said as they walked out.

I felt a combination of embarrassment and anger. This is not a scene we should witness in the world's richest and most powerful industrialized country. The sad truth, however, is that such scenes are played out hundreds of times a day across the United States; nearly 46 million Americans have no insurance. And, indeed, any of us could face their situation. All it takes is the loss of a job, a serious illness, or a little bad luck. No one with insurance can afford to be complacent about the cost of his or her health care.

This is the third book in a series I have written for Times Books/Henry Holt. The first was on retirement, the second on financial planning. Both discuss tactics for having a better life on less money than perhaps many people think they can. Both offer a clear, optimistic path to freedom from worries about money. Because of the nature of our health-care system, however, the choices in this book often involve picking the least onerous of several not-so-great options.

America's health-care system is in transition: The old employer-based insurance plans, which have many failings, are crumbling around us; whatever will replace them is a decade or more away. Many low-income workers don't get coverage at their jobs, can't afford to pay for individual coverage, and don't qualify for public assistance programs. More and more people, especially as they get older, can't qualify for individual insurance because of preexisting health conditions. In the meantime, things are likely to get worse before they get better. Many so-called solutions—health savings accounts, high-deductible plans, bare-bones policies, plans that force the sick to pay more for insurance than the healthy—do very little to get at the core problems, including soaring medical costs; some may end up exacerbating them.

Health Care on Less Than You Think is a guide for dealing with our increasingly dysfunctional health-care system in the coming years. My goal is to help average people cope with the increasingly disastrous, dangerous, and wasteful U.S. health-care system and to be prepared to protect their finances against health costs as the system continues to worsen, which is widely predicted. This means learning how to make smart choices about selecting and finding insurance coverage and knowing how to get the best insurance for your money and the maximum benefits from your policy. It also means understanding what your options are if you are having trouble getting insurance or have been rejected. Each of this book's chapters will deal with these and related issues, including help in deciding if health savings accounts are for you, finding prescription drugs at the lowest prices, and coping with the confusion surrounding the new Medicare drug coverage. In short, this book will help you make the best choices in a constantly shifting landscape. Despite the growing problems, there are things you can do to make yourself more secure and to lessen the chances of being swept away financially in the brewing health-care storm in America.

Health Care on Less Than You Think

Spending More, Getting Less

The American health-care system is collapsing around us.

—FORMER SENATOR JOHN B. BREAUX

The health-care crisis that is engulfing workers is by far the most important and difficult domestic issue facing the United States today. According to a 2005 poll by the Kaiser Family Foundation, a non-profit health-policy research group based in Menlo Park, California, Americans ranked health care behind only war and foreign policy—and just ahead of the economy—as the most important issue for the government to address. No wonder. Our system is in shambles, and the near-term prognosis for fixing it is not good. Workers whose insurance is provided by their employers face constant cuts in coverage and increases in costs that threaten their savings. The 76 million baby boomers are beginning to retire and are likely to stretch Medicare's budget to the breaking point; Medicaid, the government health-care program for the poor, is in critical condition in many states. Still more dire, the ranks of the uninsured—between 45.8 million and 81.8 million, depending on whether those with sporadic coverage are counted—continue to swell. Given the nature of the

American political system, things are certain to get much worse over the next decade or so before they get better.

Understanding how we got into this mess is important to getting out of it, so this chapter looks at the broad systemic problems of American's health-care system. The central aim of this book, however, is to help you deal with the system as it is—not as it was or might be—so if you'd like to go directly to practical matters, skip ahead. You can always return to this chapter later.

HOW BAD IS THE CRISIS?

If you have a job and your employer provides comprehensive health insurance, you probably have access to pretty good care. You have some choice in selecting your doctor, you can usually get an appointment in a matter of days, and if you are hospitalized you can be reasonably confident your care will meet certain minimal standards. You also have some peace of mind in knowing that most of your medical bills will be paid. Yet that care is likely not as good as you have been led to believe. If you have a serious illness or accident, your pretty good health insurance may leave you responsible for some pretty big bills. America is facing a health-care crisis not simply because so many lack insurance; we have cobbled together an irrational and inefficient system that is filled with loopholes, obstacles, and unmarked hazards even for those with insurance.

Many Americans think our health-care system is the best in the world. Unfortunately, this is no longer true. For certain expensive, high-technology surgical procedures, medical care in the United States is unrivaled. But this is only a small portion of the overall medical picture. Much of the rest is an increasingly dysfunctional system the benefits of which don't come close to matching its outrageous expense. Its failure is not just hurting the health of our citizens but is a drag on our economy.

Because most people get health insurance through their employers, the spiraling costs of health care have been cited in layoffs, bankruptcies, and announcements of low profits or losses. The chief executive of General Motors—where annual health-care costs approach $6 billion or an estimated $1,500 per vehicle, more than the cost of steel—warns that "the health-care crisis is putting our future at stake." The chairman of Starbucks, whose company spends more on employee health insurance than it spends on the raw materials needed to brew its coffee, calls the situation "completely non-sustainable." The costs are squeezing American companies that compete with companies from countries whose citizens have guaranteed national health care that is less expensive and—better for the bottom line—not provided directly by employers. Toyota recently decided to locate a new plant in Canada instead of Alabama, partly because of savings the automaker will enjoy under that country's national health insurance. GM, which operates several plants in Canada, has lobbied the Canadian government not to change its national health-care system. As Dr. Arnold S. Relman, a Harvard Medical School professor emeritus and former editor of the *New England Journal of Medicine,* wrote in the March 7, 2005, issue of the *New Republic,* rising health costs "are threatening the financial stability and competitiveness of many American businesses and are discouraging the hiring of new full-time workers."

Employer-based insurance also has unpleasant consequences for workers. Those who would like to change jobs, retire early, or start their own business are often unable to do so because they fear losing health coverage or being unable to afford it on their own. (We'll look at the problem of so-called job lock and its consequences in chapter 3.)

To get a handle on how little we are getting for our health-care dollars, first consider infant mortality rates—one of several common, universally accepted measures for ranking nations on the quality and availability of their health services. According to the *CIA World Factbook*—yes, the Central Intelligence Agency, not some dewy-eyed liberal group—the United States' estimated 2005 rate of infant deaths per thousand live births stands at 6.5, giving 41 countries out of 224 a ranking higher than America. Even impoverished Cuba stands two notches above the United States, with an infant mortality rate of 6.33. Most industrialized nations have better infant mortality rates than America. Singapore tops the list at 2.29. As a whole, the European Union's rate is 5.1. Nicholas D. Kristof, an op-ed columnist for the *New York Times*, noted in a January 12, 2005, column that if the United States had an infant mortality rate only as good as Cuba's, we could save an additional 2,212 babies a year; with a rate as good as Singapore's, we could save 18,900 babies a year.

The more data you look at, the worse it gets. Life expectancy at birth in the United States stands at 77.71 years, ranking 47 out of 224 countries. Tiny Andorra tops the list at 83.51 years, with Singapore, Hong Kong, and Japan all hitting over 81 years, and the European Union, overall, standing at 78.3 years.

The World Health Organization ranks the United States thirty-seventh in terms of overall health performance; in fairness of health care, it ranks fifty-fourth.

A study published several years ago in the *Journal of the American Medical Association* by Dr. Barbara Starfield, a physician and distinguished professor at the Johns Hopkins Bloomberg School of Public Health, compared health conditions in the United States with those of twelve other leading industrialized countries. The United States ranked an average of twelfth for the sixteen health indicators examined. It was in last place for low birth weights, neonatal and infant mortality overall, and years of life lost. It edged up for life expectancy at the age of one for females (ranking eleventh) and for males (ranking twelfth) and for life expectancy at the age of fifteen for females (ranking tenth) and for males (again, ranking twelfth). At the time of the study, Japan ranked highest among developed countries in terms of health; France has since moved into that spot. Starfield points out that the United States tends to rank worse each year.

Starfield cited two causes behind America's poor showing: the huge numbers of people without insurance and a weak primary-care system. She said that while Americans without insurance, as well as many covered by Medicaid, are not getting good primary care, the same is true for a lot of people with insurance. That's because people often go directly to specialists. "We have a notion in this country that if you want to go to a specialist, you should be able to do that," she said. "In fact, that doesn't assure you the best care. Our research shows that the more specialists in a given area, the worse the health. The average person would have better health if he or she had better primary care instead of so much specialty care. Specialty care is important, but when it's appropriate." In her JAMA article, Starfield points out that of the seven countries in the top of the average health ranking, five have strong primary-care infrastructures. "Although better access to care, including universal health insurance, is widely considered to be the solution, there is evidence that the major benefit of access accrues only when it facilitates receipt of primary care," she states.

Other critics have cited the boom in managed care and health maintenance organizations in the 1980s and 1990s for reducing the quality of primary care by pressuring physicians to see more patients for shorter periods of time. Indeed, surveys and polls show substantial levels of dissatisfaction with the quality of the U.S. health-care system by both patients and doctors.

Here are some other health statistics that people who have always thought of American medical care as the best in the world might find jolting.

- A University of California study projects that by 2013, one in four American workers under the age of sixty-five—nearly 56 million people—will be uninsured.
- Nearly 20 percent—8.4 million—of the 45.8 million people the government says have no health insurance are children, according to the Robert Wood Johnson Foundation. The foundation says that 70 percent of the uninsured children would be eligible for free or

low-cost coverage under Medicaid or the State Children's Health Insurance Program, know as SCHIP, but many parents are unaware of the programs or too overwhelmed by the paperwork and bureaucracy to apply for them.

• Lack of health insurance causes 18,000 unnecessary deaths a year, according to the National Academy of Sciences. (Some health-care experts think the 18,000 total is too conservative.) Of those deaths, about 1,400 are due to unidentified and undertreated high blood pressure; approximately 500 are among women with breast cancer; and about 1,350 are among HIV-infected adults. By way of comparison, diabetes accounts for between 15,000 and 16,000 deaths each year.

• Women are 70 percent more likely to die in childbirth in America than in Europe, according to data from the government, the thirty-nation Organization for Economic Cooperation and Development,* and the United Nations. This is in large part because many pregnant women without health insurance receive no prenatal care; by the time they show up at an emergency room to have their children, problems that could have been dealt with along the way have become full-blown crises.

• Uninsured adults are twenty-five times more likely to die prematurely than their insured counterparts, according to the National Academy of Sciences.

The insured don't have it easy either:

• A 2005 survey by the Commonwealth Fund—a private foundation supporting research on health and social issues—of seven thousand sick adults in the United States, Australia, Canada, New Zealand,

*The members of the OECD are: Australia, Austria, Belgium, Canada, the Czech Republic, Denmark, Finland, France, Germany, Greece, Hungary, Iceland, Ireland, Italy, Japan, Luxembourg, Mexico, the Netherlands, New Zealand, Norway, Poland, Portugal, the Slovak Republic, South Korea, Spain, Sweden, Switzerland, Turkey, the United Kingdom, and the United States.

Great Britain, and Germany found that nearly a third of American patients reported spending more than $1,000 a year in out-of-pocket expenses for their care. Canadians and Australians were next, with 14 percent reporting spending that much. More than half of the Americans went without needed care because of costs, and more than one-third cited mistakes and disorganized care when they did get treated.

· Almost half of personal bankruptcies in the United States stem from overwhelming medical bills, according to research by Harvard Law School and Harvard Medical School. Of those filing for medical bankruptcy, more than 75 percent had health insurance at the start of the bankrupting illness.

· Medical errors are higher in the United States, even for patients with insurance, than for patients in several countries that have state-funded systems, according to a 2005 study by the Commonwealth Fund. Over a two-year period, 34 percent of U.S. patients encountered a medical mistake, compared with 30 percent in Canada. Error rates were also lower in Great Britain, Australia, Germany, and New Zealand.

· In 2005, for the first time, the cost of health insurance in the United States for a family of four surpassed the total before-tax income of a minimum wage worker.

It's little wonder that when the Commonwealth Fund conducted a survey of health policies of several countries in 2002 (figure 1), it found a clear relationship between costs and lack of health care.

All these comparisons are, of course, much worse when we look at only poor and minority groups. According to United Nations figures:

· Black infants in Washington, D.C., have a higher death rate than infants in the Indian state of Kerala.

· Hispanic Americans are more than twice as likely as white Americans to lack health coverage.

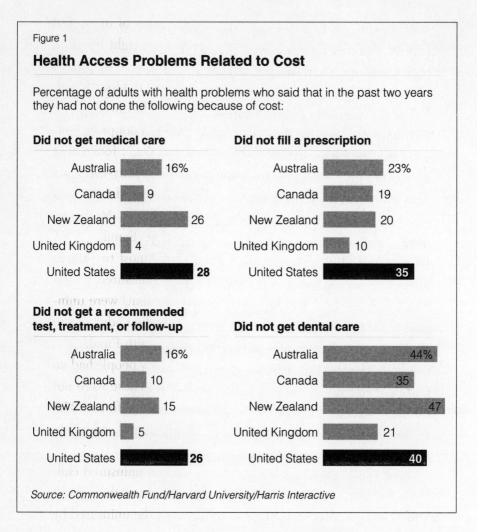

Figure 1

Health Access Problems Related to Cost

Percentage of adults with health problems who said that in the past two years they had not done the following because of cost:

Did not get medical care

Australia	16%
Canada	9
New Zealand	26
United Kingdom	4
United States	**28**

Did not fill a prescription

Australia	23%
Canada	19
New Zealand	20
United Kingdom	10
United States	**35**

Did not get a recommended test, treatment, or follow-up

Australia	16%
Canada	10
New Zealand	15
United Kingdom	5
United States	**26**

Did not get dental care

Australia	44%
Canada	35
New Zealand	47
United Kingdom	21
United States	40

Source: Commonwealth Fund/Harvard University/Harris Interactive

- If the gap in health care between black and white Americans were closed, it would save nearly eighty-five thousand lives a year.

UNINSURED AND UNDERINSURED

These disturbing data are the inevitable consequence of the large number of Americans who lack insurance—or lack enough insurance to cover their medical bills, especially when a major illness or accident strikes. The U.S. Census Bureau put the number of uninsured at 45.8 million for 2004, an increase of more than eight hundred thousand from 2003, but counted only those who were uninsured for the entire year. (The report for 2004 represented the fourth consecutive year of increases; the number of uninsured has swelled by 6 million since 2000.) A 2004 study by Families USA, a nonprofit consumer health organization based in Washington, D.C., found that 81.8 million people—a third of the population under sixty-five years old—lacked health insurance at some point in 2002 and 2003, and most of those were uninsured for more than nine months. Medicare, of course, covers people sixty-five and older. The Families USA study, based mainly on census data, showed that almost two-thirds of those lacking insurance (65.3 percent) were uninsured for six months or more; slightly more than half (50.6 percent) were uninsured for at least nine months. In addition, 16 million adults were *underinsured* in 2003, according to the Commonwealth Fund.

In fourteen states, more than a third of nonelderly people had no health insurance for all or part of 2002 and 2003. These were not just poor states; they included Texas (43.4 percent), California (37.1 percent), Nevada (36.8 percent), Alaska (35.0 percent), and New York (33.4 percent).

And while there is much talk and concern about uninsured children, lack of health insurance is a problem for Americans throughout their prime working years. Here is a breakdown of the uninsured by age, according to Families USA.

AGE	PERCENTAGE
0 to 17	36.7
18 to 24	50.3
25 to 44	32.9
45 to 54	20.7
55 to 64	17.3

Lack of health insurance is not just a problem of the poor or un-employed. The great majority of the uninsured—nearly 83 percent—live in families headed by workers, according to a study of 2004 census data by the Employee Benefit Research Institute, a nonprofit and nonpartisan policy organization based in Washington, D.C. Of working families, according to Families USA, significant portions of the middle class were found to be uninsured. For example, among people with annual incomes between 300 and 400 percent of the federal poverty level (between $55,980 and $74,640 for a family of four in 2003), more than one out of four were uninsured. Even among families with annual incomes of $75,000 and up, 13.5 million people were without insurance for part of 2002 and 2003. In its study, the Employee Benefit Research Institute also found that nearly 63 percent of all uninsured workers were self-employed or working for private-sector companies with fewer than a hundred employees.

In an analysis of the Census Bureau report for 2004, the nonprofit Physicians for a National Health Program (PNHP) found that middle-class Americans with annual incomes between $50,000 and $75,000 were the fastest-growing group of uninsured, accounting for 616,000 of the more than 800,000 that were added to the rolls in 2004. "The high cost of insurance premiums [is] forcing millions of middle-class Americans to forgo coverage, and millions more find that their skimpy policies leave them vulnerable to high out-of-pocket costs and even bankruptcy if they are seriously ill," said Dr. David Himmelstein, an associate professor of medicine at Harvard Medical School and a cofounder of PNHP.

According to Ron Pollack, the executive director of Families USA: "The growing problem of Americans without health insurance is now a phenomenon that significantly affects middle-class and working families. As a result, this problem is no longer simply an altruistic issue affecting the poor, but a matter of self-interest for almost everyone."

Two other major studies support the conclusion by Families USA that the Census Bureau understates the problem of the uninsured.

One of the reasons health insurance premiums are so high is that many medical bills include what amounts to a hidden or obscured surcharge to help pay for the treatment of the nearly 46 million Americans who are uninsured. Those without health insurance often cannot afford the preventive or primary care they would receive in a relatively low-cost office visit and usually put off seeking treatment until their medical problems are more advanced—and thus more difficult and costly to treat. Indeed, they often show up in expensive hospital emergency rooms for conditions that could have been handled earlier at a fraction of the cost. About a third of the cost of this care is paid by the uninsured themselves. Government programs pay about 20 percent; most of the remaining amount, about $43 billion each year, is covered through higher charges to those with health insurance. The situation will worsen as more people join the ranks of the uninsured. At the beginning of 2006, for example, employers in Maine faced a 2 percent increase in premiums for their workers because of a fee assessed by the state to fund health coverage for the uninsured. Families USA points out that as the costs of care for the uninsured are added to already expensive and steeply rising premiums, employers are more likely to increase employee health costs or drop coverage altogether. That creates a vicious cycle.

THE PRICE TAG

The really galling part of America's shameful rankings is that we pay more—a lot more—for health care than countries that outrank us. It's like adding insult to injury: We get less, and it's more expensive.

According to Families USA, premiums for families who have coverage through their private employers are getting higher precisely because of the cost of health care for the uninsured that is not paid by the uninsured themselves or some other source. In six states, health insurance for families was at least $1,500 higher—which can represent as much as 15 percent or more of a family's premiums—in 2005 than it would have been due to the unreimbursed costs of care for the uninsured:

New Mexico	$1,875
West Virginia	1,796
Oklahoma	1,781
Montana	1,578
Texas	1,551
Arkansas	1,514

For individuals, employer coverage was an average of $341 higher in 2005 because of the uninsured. The increase topped $500 in the following eight states:

New Mexico	$726
Oklahoma	680
West Virginia	660
Montana	594
Alaska	565
Arkansas	560
Idaho	551
Texas	550

By 2010, Families USA projects, family premiums will average $1,502 higher because of the uninsured. The increase will exceed $2,000 in these eleven states:

New Mexico	$3,169
West Virginia	2,940

Oklahoma	2,911
Texas	2,786
Arkansas	2,748
Alaska	2,248
Florida	2,248
Montana	2,190
Idaho	2,152
Washington	2,144
Arizona	2,028

For individuals, the 2010 premium will be an average of $532 more because of the uninsured. The increase will surpass $800 in these eight states:

New Mexico	$1,192
Oklahoma	1,127
West Virginia	1,037
Arkansas	943
Texas	922
Alaska	857
Idaho	820
Montana	807

Surcharges are only the beginning. According to a study by Boston University, about half of our health-care spending is eaten up by waste, excessive prices, and fraud. And we're talking about big bucks here: For 2004, U.S. spending on health care reached $1.9 trillion and consumed 16 percent of the economy, up from 13.2 percent in 2002, according to government figures. The Boston University study also found that U.S. health spending per person is twice the average of such spending in Canada, France, Germany, Italy, and Great Britain—countries that guarantee health care for all their citizens. The most recent data for the top thirty industrialized nations show that the United States spent $5,635 per capita for health care in 2003. That's $1,828, or 48 percent, more than Switzerland, which has the second-highest per-capita spending, and more than double the median OECD country. "Current U.S. spending should be adequate to cover all Americans," the Boston University study concludes. The bottom line: If our system were more efficient, less greedy, and honest, we could cover everyone with the savings.

Gerard F. Anderson, a professor at the Johns Hopkins Bloomberg School of Public Health, asks the simple question: Why is our health care so expensive? Conventional wisdom holds that other countries save money by maintaining frustratingly long waiting lists for elective procedures and that the United States is plagued by malpractice lawsuits that drive up our medical costs. In the July–August 2005 issue of *Health Affairs*, Anderson and his colleagues demonstrate this is simply not the case.

The *Health Affairs* article points out that per-capita spending for the seven top industrial countries that do not have waiting lists for elective surgery averaged $2,696, only a little above the $2,366 average for those with waiting lists, and both, of course, were much less than the U.S. average of more than $5,000. They also note that "procedures for which waiting lists exist in some countries represent a small part of total health spending."

As for malpractice suits, Anderson and his colleagues calculate that the expense of defending malpractice claims—including awards, legal costs, and underwriting costs—equals less than 0.5 percent of the United States' total spending on health care. The authors concede that "defensive" medicine, such as tests or procedures ordered primarily to protect medical providers against the risk of being sued, contribute to health spending possibly more than malpractice payments themselves. But they emphasize that this is hard to quantify; seemingly defensive procedures could also be medically appropriate.

So why does medical care cost more in America? "It's expensive because our prices are higher," Anderson said. "We charge a lot. It's pretty simple." In fact, Anderson and his colleagues cite research that shows "the prices of care, not the amount of care delivered, are the primary difference between the United States and other countries." These higher prices are increasingly making health care unaffordable for many Americans. Even when factoring in higher U.S. incomes and costs of living, our per-capita medical costs, according to Anderson and his colleagues, are still $2,037 higher than these factors would predict. Here's another surprise: In terms of hospital beds, physicians and nurses, magnetic resonance imaging (MRI) scanners, and computed tomography (CT) scanners, Americans have access to fewer health-care resources on a per-capita basis than people in many other industrialized countries—despite our much higher costs (see figure 2).

There is, of course, a caveat about comparing the data in figure 2, particularly regarding the numbers of MRI units and CT scanners in a country: The authors suggest that the United States may use its relatively low supply of these machines more efficiently than other countries. "For example, lengths of hospital stay are generally shorter and more intense, and CT and MRI scanners may be used more frequently than in other countries," they note. "The greater intensity of care could explain why the United States has fewer health care resources and pays higher prices for their use."

Nevertheless, these various comparisons should at least give pause to proponents of the medical status quo here. I used to live in Europe and received medical care through the government systems in Belgium, France, and Great Britain. In no case did I ever feel slighted in quality of care. In fact, the doctors in these countries routinely make house calls to people who are shut-ins or otherwise have trouble getting to a doctor's office. That kind of service is simply not available any more in most of America. Premiums are going up, the number of uninsured is rising, and we get less health care for more money.

It has been my experience that defenders of the current system are almost always members of the well-insured class. As we shall see

Figure 2

Comparing Quality of Care

Country	Per thousand people:			Per million people:	
	Hospital beds	Physicians	Nurses	MRI units	CT scanners
Australia	3.7	2.5	10.4	4.7	–
Austria	6.1	3.3	9.3	13.4	27.3
Belgium	–	3.9	5.6	–	–
Canada	3.2	2.1	9.4	4.2	9.7
Czech Republic	**6.5**	3.5	9.4	2.2	12.1
Denmark	3.4	3.3	9.7	8.6	13.8
Finland	2.3	3.1	9.0	12.5	13.3
France	4.0	3.3	7.2	2.7	9.7
Germany	–	3.3	9.9	5.5	13.3
Greece	4.0	**4.5**	4.0	2.4	17.7
Hungary	5.9	3.2	8.5	2.5	6.8
Iceland	–	3.6	14.0	17.4	20.9
Ireland	3.0	2.4	**15.3**	–	–
Italy	4.6	4.4	5.4	10.4	23.0
Japan	–	2.0	8.2	**35.3**	**92.6**
Luxembourg	5.8	2.6	10.8	4.5	24.7
Mexico	1.0	1.5	2.2	1.1	2.6
Netherlands	3.3	3.1	12.8	–	–
New Zealand	–	2.1	9.4	–	11.2
Norway	3.1	3.0	10.4	–	–
Poland	4.6	2.3	4.8	–	–
Portugal	3.2	3.2	3.8	–	–
Slovak Republic	5.5	3.6	7.1	2.0	10.6
South Korea	5.7	1.5	1.7	7.9	30.9
Spain	2.8	2.9	7.1	6.2	12.8
Sweden	2.4	3.0	8.8	7.9	14.2
Switzerland	3.9	3.6	10.7	14.1	18.0
Turkey	2.1	1.3	1.7	3.0	7.5
United Kingdom	3.9	2.1	9.2	4.0	5.8
United States	**2.9**	**2.4**	**7.9**	**8.2***	**12.8***
OECD median	**3.7**	**3.1**	**8.9**	**5.5**	**13.3**

A dash indicates that figures were not available.

*United States statistics may undercount the number of MRI units and CT scanners at locations where more than one unit is installed.

Source: Organization for Economic Cooperation and Development

in chapter 2, however, those who think they are financially protected by insurance may discover otherwise when a costly illness strikes.

HOW DID WE GET IN THIS FIX?

The history of health care in the United States is mainly a story of missed opportunities, often for reasons totally unrelated to health or care. Although there were calls for health-care reform and universal coverage during the Progressive era of the early twentieth century, the seeds of our current crisis were sown in the 1940s. Before then, people paid for their own health insurance or paid their medical bills directly.

The tight labor market during World War II changed that. "During the Second World War, when there was a severe labor shortage, along with wage and price controls, companies starting offering employee insurance as a way to give workers a 'raise,'" explained Leif Wellington Haase, a health-care fellow at the Century Foundation in New York. "Doing it this way became embedded in our system." Companies, however, have never been required to offer insurance; nor does the system cover those who cannot work or who are self-employed. Yet so many people started to receive insurance as a job benefit that it eventually helped to give rise to giant, powerful insurance and health-care companies. Arnold Relman of Harvard Medical School dubbed the system the "new medical-industrial complex," echoing President Dwight D. Eisenhower's warning about the rise of the military-industrial complex.

While the United States expanded its ad hoc system of employer-based health coverage after World War II, European nations took a different path. They established medical care as a right, not a privilege, and guaranteed coverage for all their citizens. The "universal coverage" concept enjoys broad support across the political spectrum in Europe. Some countries, like Great Britain, established a single-payer, government-run system; other nations adopted highly regulated public-private arrangements. In all cases, however, citizens were covered regardless of their employment situations.

One of the first major efforts to change America's course and establish universal coverage came immediately after World War II when President Harry S. Truman tried to create a national health insurance system in 1945. At the time, it was supported by 75 percent of Americans. The effort, however, failed mainly because of opposition from powerful special-interest groups including the American Medical Association, which once opposed any kind of insurance coverage at all. In her book *One Nation, Uninsured* (Oxford University Press, 2005), Jill Quadagno suggests that Truman was also up against powerful southern politicians who feared that national coverage would lead to racially integrated hospitals.

Two decades after Truman failed to win passage of universal health care, President Lyndon B. Johnson flew to Independence, Missouri, and, with the former president at his side, signed the legislation that created Medicare—providing health care for the elderly and disabled—and Medicaid—providing it for the poor. The American Medical Association fought Medicare, calling it "a deception and a danger that would threaten the relationship between patients and doctors." Henry J. Aaron, a senior fellow at the Brookings Institution, recalled that "the head of the AMA even likened his group's fight against Medicare to Winston Churchill's stand against the Nazis."

The AMA's lobbying power, however, was slipping, and being overtaken by that of giant insurance companies. Quadagno suggests in *One Nation, Uninsured* that Medicare and Medicaid passed into law because the programs fund care for "groups—the aged and the very poor—that private insurers have no desire to cover." Despite its critics, its funding problems, and its coverage gaps, Medicare—which we'll look at in detail in chapter 8—became one of the great success stories of the twentieth century. "In the years leading up to Medicare, the private market was simply not working for older Americans," said Robert M. Hayes, the president of the Medicare Rights Center, which helps individuals deal with Medicare-related problems. "Life is so much better for millions of Americans because of Medicare."

In 1972, the Medicare Act was amended by Congress to cover people, regardless of their age or income, who suffered from kidney failure and needed dialysis treatments to survive. Prior to the amendment, many people with end-stage renal disease who couldn't afford expensive dialysis treatments died; there were simply not enough machines and money to go around. Then-Senator Vance Hartke of Indiana summed up the rationale for the new law: "In what must be the most tragic irony of the twentieth century, people are dying because they cannot get access to proper medical care. We have learned how to treat or cure some of the diseases that have plagued mankind for centuries, yet those treatments are not available because of their costs." As a result of the amendment, about three hundred thousand patients receive dialysis at more than four thousand clinics around the country today.

Late in 2003, the Congress again successfully amended Medicare, this time to include limited, voluntary coverage for prescription drugs—a program that began in January 2006. The Medicare Part D plan attempted to graft the private insurance industry onto the government program in order to deal with a massive shift in health care: a growing preference for pharmaceutical treatments for many medical conditions. The benefits, however, have so far been relatively puny; the program did not allow the government to negotiate drug prices and thus did not control costs. The plan also became infamous for its complexity. The confusion led many seniors to put off enrollment; fewer initially signed up for the plan than had been expected. (A lot of Washington watchers predict that the legislation will have to be revisited sooner rather than later by Congress.)

Even with these expansions in Medicare, America's health-care system remained haphazard, provided mainly at the whim of employers. Leif Haase of the Century Foundation points out that the employer-based coverage for the bulk of the population was tolerable to companies for the first forty years or so because costs were relatively low and could usually be passed on to the consumer in the form of modest price increases. Look back to 1980 when total U.S. health care spending was only about $250 billion; costs are now approaching $2 trillion, more than the gross domestic product of Great Britain or France. "That's about a fivefold increase in real, inflation-adjusted terms since 1980. Just since 2000, health costs for employers have soared fifty-nine percent," Haase said—"a remarkable jump." Along the way, America turned to managed care and HMOs to try to stop the hemorrhaging. "They thought they had a magic bullet to control costs," Haase said. "That hasn't worked out."

And with more problems have come more fixes—and failures. Another big, but ill-fated, push for national health care came from President Bill Clinton in the early 1990s. Like the system it was trying to reform, the Clinton plan was vastly complex and depended on employer-based insurance. It failed, depending on whom you listen to, because (a) too many special-interest groups (i.e., big insurers) were excluded during the planning stages or (b) it was overly accommodating of too many special-interest groups (i.e., big insurers). In 1998, during his second term, Clinton proposed allowing uninsured Americans between ages fifty-five and sixty-four to enroll in Medicare for $3,600 to $5,000 a year, depending on their age—a so-called Medicare buy-in. That proposal, which would have especially benefited early retirees, went nowhere in the Republican-controlled Congress. After the Clinton failure, health-care reform was relatively dormant for a decade. Nevertheless, the problems continued to build. Price increases for health services outpaced inflation, and the number of uninsured swelled.

A little-noticed amendment to the 2003 Medicare drug bill created health savings accounts (HSAs), part of President George W. Bush's push for "consumer-directed" health care in what he envisions as an "ownership" society (which also includes partial privatization of Social Security). HSAs combine less-expensive high-deductible insurance policies with 401(k)-type savings accounts that can be used to pay the deductibles. These policies are advantageous for some, as we shall see in chapter 4, but do nothing to address the problems of people who cannot afford to pay premiums, even if they are less, nor do they help people who can't get insurance because of preexisting conditions.

Leif Haase thinks this latest fix does not go far enough in breaking the link between health insurance and jobs. "Now they are pushing consumer-directed health plans," he said, "but as the problems of this approach become apparent, we might get something more comprehensive." In other words, managed care has failed and is now being replaced by consumer-directed plans (read: plans that shift more costs to consumers). Haase believes that once *these* plans fail to pull down the costs of health care, there will be few other options. Employers will want out of the system, and over the next ten years things are likely to get worse before they get better. "When the private market wears itself out, we'll have to turn to something more rational," Haase said. "In the process, we will have exhausted the centers of power in the medical establishment, including insurance companies. The medical establishment will no longer be able to dictate the terms."

Relman agrees with Haase's prognosis. In his *New Republic* article titled "The Health of Nations: Medicine and the Free Market," Relman writes: "The start of substantial reform will probably have to wait for CDHC [consumer-driven health care] to play itself out, just as investor-owned managed care did in the last decade. . . . I expect the system to become so dysfunctional, and costs to become so onerous, that the availability of services to the poor will reach scandalous proportions. At that juncture, public opinion will probably demand that health care move from market control to some form of government protection and guaranteed benefits. Major reform of our entire health care system might then become a politically realistic option."

At least one insurance executive agrees: Stephen L. Wyss, managing director of Affinity Group Underwriters in Glen Allen, Virginia, which provides life, health, and disability insurance for professional organizations. "None of these plans—whether managed care or health savings accounts—deal with the problem of people with preexisting conditions or with those who can't afford to pay," Wyss said. "They are just nibbling around the edges of the problem."

If health costs are such a strain on corporations, why don't they use their political clout to push for a different system? They might, especially as their costs continue to increase. Today, more than 160 million Americans get their coverage through their employers; it's tax free for the employees and tax deductible for their employers. Yet, on the other side of the equation, studies have clearly shown that workers with continuous health insurance miss significantly less work than their uninsured counterparts. Wyss says he is surprised companies haven't publicly moved to end the employer-based system, but thinks they will. "In fact," he said, "I think they are lobbying, just not publicly. One of the reasons the system will change is the collapse of the employer-based health-care system. Companies are going to say, 'Wait a minute. Who elected us to do this? We quit.' After all, the extra taxes companies might have to pay to help support national health insurance would be less than their current insurance costs and would be predictable." In fact, in 2005 the *New York Times* disclosed that leaders representing the health-care industry, corporations, unions, and conservative and liberal groups had been meeting secretly for months to seek a consensus on proposals to provide coverage for the growing number of people with no health insurance.

REFORMING THE SYSTEM

When will real change and improvement take place? Leif Haase of the Century Foundation believes the health-care system will be reconfigured in the next ten years or so. Other experts think that time line is optimistic.

Whatever reforms take hold must address two major issues that our current system has proved unable to handle. First, they must control the soaring costs of health care in America as compared with the rest of the industrialized world, which has equal or better care. Second, coverage must be accessible to nonseniors with preexisting medical conditions who currently can find themselves shut off from affordable coverage.

It's interesting to note that in the decades since Truman's 1945 proposal—and despite the rightward swing of America in recent years—the percentage of Americans who favor national health insurance has not changed much. An October 2005 bipartisan poll for former senator John B. Breaux's Ceasefire on Health Care campaign found that 74 percent favored guaranteeing that every American citizen receives health care. A poll the previous month by Harris Interactive found that 75 percent of adults favored universal health insurance. The clamor for universal coverage even made it to the cover of *Business Week* magazine in 2005. In its accompanying article, *Business Week* cited a 2004 survey by the Civil Society Institute, a nonprofit group based in Massachusetts, which found 67 percent of Americans favored guaranteed health care; only 27 percent disagreed. A 2004 Kaiser Family Foundation survey found that 76 percent either strongly agreed (48 percent) or somewhat agreed (28 percent) that health care should be a right; only 10 percent strongly disagreed. In January 2006, a *New York Times*/CBS News poll found that 90 percent of Americans think the U.S. health-care system needs fundamental changes or needs to be completely rebuilt. And a month earlier, a statewide poll by the *Arizona Republic* found widespread support for universal health care, with 81 percent of registered voters surveyed in that politically conservative state saying it is time that the state or federal government step in and create a health-care system that ensures everyone has access to medical care.

What kind of system could cut costs and guarantee coverage? For one case study, we can go over our northern border. The Canadian system, created in 1966, is a single-payer government-run plan that bans private health insurance for services provided through its coverage. Canada's health care, which does not cover prescription drugs, has come under a lot of criticism lately, much of it from Americans who don't want to see a similar system built in the United States. But it faces its own challenges. In 2005, Canada's Supreme Court struck down the ban on private insurance in Quebec province. Although the ruling applies only to Quebec, it is sure to lead to copycat cases in other provinces and give impetus to a growing movement for a combination of public and private care in the country. Supporters of the status quo in Canada fear a two-tier health system: private care for the rich and government care for everyone else.

There's actually a good reason for having everyone enrolled in the same system. It's to avoid *adverse selection.* Insurance companies sometimes are loath to concede it, but the whole idea behind insurance of any kind is that everyone in a large group pays small amounts into a fund that then reimburses members who have a problem, whether it's illness, injury, property loss, or death. The larger the group, the more representative it is of the entire population. Some people may pay premiums and never collect benefits, while others may get sick or have bad luck and wind up collecting a lot. No matter; the risk is spread over the whole group and does not fall heavily on any one person or subset of people.

Insurance companies, of course, would like to insure only people at low risk for getting sick; that practice is called *cherry-picking.* But what insurers really seek is to avoid insuring a group of people who have a high risk of getting sick. This is adverse selection.

The problem of adverse selection led directly to the creation of Medicare. When insurance companies stopped underwriting the medical care of older Americans, Medicare became a necessity. Medicare is by definition adversely select in that it insures only those over age sixty-five—who are less healthy than the entire population on average—and the disabled. Yet within that group, all are treated the same; Medicare does not reject anyone or charge its healthier members less than its sicker ones. In fact, partly to avoid adverse selection within the sixty-five-plus population Medicare insures, all Americans are, by law, covered by Medicare Part A, which pays for hospital care. One of the advantages of a national single-payer system like Canada's is that it completely bypasses the hazard of adverse selection; the whole country is the group. The Canadians who fear the entrée of private insurance worry that it would leave the government insuring only a poorer, less healthy group at a higher price.

Dr. Barbara Starfield, the Johns Hopkins professor who ranked health conditions in industrialized countries, favors a single-payer system that covers everyone, regardless of employment or medical condition. She contends it would cut costs by a third, whether run by the government or by a heavily regulated private entity such as a trust or foundation. She is opposed to copayments and coinsurance. "They are a barrier for people to get basic primary care," she said. "They cut down on necessary and unnecessary care equally and work against people who can afford them least."

There are disadvantages to a national single-payer system—especially if you are wealthy. Many of the complaints about Canada's health system involve waits for elective procedures. Some of these critics seem to argue that it's better to be uninsured than have to wait for elective care.

In fact, waits, sometimes long ones, are part of most health-care systems, including America's, particularly in urban areas—and sometimes for emergency as well as nonemergency care. A 2002 Commonwealth Fund survey found that 31 percent of those polled in the United States said waiting time for emergency care was a big problem; the figure was 28 percent for New Zealand, 31 percent for Australia, 36 percent for Great Britain, and 37 percent for Canada. It's not uncommon to spend ten to twelve hours waiting for treatment in an overcrowded American hospital emergency room, thanks in many cases to the number of uninsured who have no place else to go when they are sick.

I recently had to wait three months to get an appointment with a specialist in Topeka, Kansas. A November 2005 study by the Commonwealth Fund looked at access to care and waiting times in the aforementioned five countries as well as Germany. The study found that American and Canadian adults with health problems were more likely to wait six days or longer for an appointment than patients in the other countries. The percentage of those receiving same-day or next-day appointments ranged from a high of 70 percent in Germany and New Zealand to below 50 percent in Canada and the United States. The divide also appeared when patients were trying to seek care after hours and on weekends.

In an August 2005 article, the *New York Times* reported that the wait for medical care in the United States has gotten worse. The *Times* wrote: "Advances in technology have created more tests and procedures to wait for, and new drugs and treatments mean more people need more doctor visits." The backup has led to the adoption of so-called concierge practices, in which wealthier patients pay an annual fee, which can range from $1,500 to $20,000, to receive prompt attention from a doctor.

A Toronto lawyer I know used to complain a lot about waiting for elective procedures in Canada. But two years ago, when he and his wife traveled to Miami for a vacation, she became ill and was taken to the emergency room of a large hospital, where she spent more than eight hours waiting to be treated. The couple was astounded that the first question they were asked at the hospital was not about the wife's condition but about how they were going to pay the bill. "That would never happen in Canada," the lawyer said. Since his experience in Miami, he has toned down his complaints about Canada's system.

MISCONCEPTIONS ABOUT CANADA'S HEALTH SYSTEM

Stephen Wyss, the managing director of Affinity Group Underwriters, praises Canada's national health system and says most people in the United States have a distorted view of it. In the insurance industry, his views stand out. But Wyss, an American who lived in Canada for nine years, argues that the health insurance problems in America are not going to be solved fully by the private sector. He thinks that Canada's system could be a model for fixing the system in the United States. But while the common misconception that Canadian patients cannot choose their doctors does not hold up, the system does not please everyone.

Some Canadian doctors complain that they would make more money in the United States. "Well, fair enough," Wyss said. But he believes the focus should be on quality of care and efficiency. "The real difference," he said, "is how the two countries pay for health care. Americans pay for it with premiums and Canadians pay for it with taxes—and cover everyone." He added, "The whole discussion in the United States about the Canadian system seems to get perverted by preconceived ideas and misconceptions about 'socialized' medicine."

That's unfortunate. Some form of national health insurance that severs the tie between where Americans work and where they get their coverage would certainly be better suited to the modern job-hopping population. The old social contracts and bonds that once existed between companies and their workers are mostly history, but the health insurance tie remains—partly due to the "socialist" misconceptions Wyss cites.

Several years ago, I heard a conservative American radio-talk-show host claim that there were only two CT-scan machines for all of Canada! Someone finally got through to him on his call-in line to correct this error, but for listeners who had switched stations or turned off the radio the damage had been done.

The same radio host later repeated stories he had heard about Canadians who were flocking to the United States for medical care, fleeing their own country's "socialized medicine." Yet a few weeks later a front-page article in the *New York Times* reported that a big problem for *Canada* was the huge number of Americans with fake Canadian medical ID cards coming north for treatment. A cottage industry had sprung up to make fake IDs for Americans without health insurance. When's the last time you heard of a busload of Canadians coming to the United States to buy prescription drugs?

While they support efforts to guarantee health care, Americans also say they don't want the government involved because it might limit or ration services. Yet the same people are often willing to accept, without a peep, draconian limitations from for-profit health insurance companies and corporations. HMOs, for example, routinely restrict patients' choice of doctors; the government-run Medicare does not. Other private insurers' restrictions can include shortened hospital stays; surgical procedures on a cheaper, outpatient basis—so-called drive-by surgery; and unrealistic caps on drugs and services. Whereas the insurance industry can impose these limits with impunity, government agencies are directly subject to political pressure from elected officials, who in turn are subject to public opinion.

More than a decade ago, my late father had coronary-bypass surgery, his second, through his Medicare HMO—a private insurer that accepted payments from the government in return for providing his medical care. The bypass was a serious operation that involved opening his chest cavity and repairing his heart while he was kept alive on a heart-lung machine. His HMO allowed him only four nights in the hospital. I picked him up on the fifth day and was appalled that he was being discharged; he clearly needed to stay in the hospital a few more days. Yet home he went, shaky and very unsteady on his feet. Luckily, his HMO did pay for a visiting-nurse service for a prescribed amount of time. Several years later, the father of a Canadian friend had similar surgery in the Toronto area. My friend's father stayed in the hospital for two weeks and then was placed in an extended-care facility for a month before he finally went home. Although both men's surgeries were successful, the difference in care is eye-opening. Who was the more caring provider, the private American insurer trying to save money on a Medicare patient or the Canadian government? Which way would you like to have your father treated? Or be treated yourself?

I'm not saying that you can't get good health care in the United States. You can. And I don't mean to imply that other countries have perfect health-care systems. They don't. The essential point I want to get across is this: For the foreseeable future, Americans don't have a very rational or caring system in place to ensure that everyone gets a more or less equal slice of the health-care pie. Like it or not, you're pretty much on your own when it comes to making sure you have the right insurance coverage and thus access to decent and affordable medical treatment. The rest of this book is aimed at helping you do just that.

2

Protect Your Health, Protect Your Budget

*Unless you're Bill Gates, you're just
one serious illness away from bankruptcy.*

—DR. DAVID HIMMELSTEIN, ASSOCIATE PROFESSOR,
HARVARD MEDICAL SCHOOL

In 2005, Dustin Block, the city editor of the *Racine Journal Times* in Wisconsin, launched a project for the newspaper Web site that, among other things, offers health-care news and a forum for people who are underinsured or have no coverage.

Block's site has received comments not only from the Racine area but from all over the country. "It's almost like people are going on-line searching for insurance sites or places to vent," Block said. (You can access the site by going to www.racinereport.com. Then, using the site's search engine, type in "health care" and click on the search button.)

Block became interested in the problems of the underinsured and uninsured after reading the book *Uninsured in America: Life and Death in the Land of Opportunity* by Susan Starr Sered and Rushika Fernandopulle (University of California Press, 2005). The book argues that the link between health insurance and employment is creating a new caste in America of the ill, infirm, and marginally employed. "Using people's stories, it describes the 'death spiral' of getting sick, not being able to work, losing insurance and not being able to get needed treatment to be able to work, which continues the cycle downward," Block writes. He adds, "The authors document not only the working poor, but also highly educated professionals who lost everything because of sickness and mounting medical bills."

Block realized that Racine, a working-class community that has been losing manufacturing jobs over the last decade and whose un-employment rate of about 10 percent is the highest in Wisconsin, was a textbook case for many of the issues described in *Uninsured in America*. "So I started asking people I would meet—my barber, the people at my laundry—about health care," Block said. "I couldn't find a person who didn't have a story about themselves or someone they know not having enough health insurance."

Here's a sampling of the voices and stories from the Web site.

My family is covered with health insurance but we still are struggling with the bills because of the lousy coverage, high cost of medical care, high deductibles, and loopholes such as "not medically neces-sary" as reasons not to pay. So even if you have coverage it's like you're paying twice because of the obnoxiously high premiums, which cut into our budget and paycheck immensely and then you're still stuck with paying a large portion of the bill. Healthcare coverage needs a major overhaul.

I'm having a hard time paying one medical bill worth $3,000. I am self-employed . . . but I don't make enough money to pay $5,000 a year for my own health coverage. I'm stuck in the middle and it sucks. I work hard, I'm a United States citizen, I shouldn't have to be afraid to get sick or go to the doctor because of the fear of receiving a medical bill I cannot afford. It's ridiculous.

I am 62 years old and in another month my health insurance will be canceled . . . I was recently dismissed from my job. I cannot get extra help from community programs because I have some funds in an IRA and a mutual fund. A person has to be totally broke or have children to get extra help or lower rates to cover health insurance. My doctor stated that women like me fall between the cracks. Thank God, I do not at this time have any serious health issues. Now I am job-hunting, and hopefully will be covered by health insurance once again. In the meantime, I pray a lot.

I had some bare-bones coverage that refused to pay for a hysterectomy two years ago, because it was "a pre-existing condition." (Go figure.) After months of arguing, I am stuck with over $30,000 in medical bills. I've also asked my doctor to take me off one of my meds because I simply can't afford them anymore. He also gave me a month's worth of samples of another med to help me out. My son's pediatrician gave samples of an antibiotic for his strep throat, because he's allergic to the affordable meds. It's impossible for small business owners to find decent, affordable healthcare.

I am one of the many Americans who don't have health insurance. When I visit the doctor (since I am a diabetic and have started having complications) I always reply to the insurance question with, "I live in America, we can't afford health insurance." I spend $500 a month for medications. I went without them for a period of time while unemployed and this led to the possibility of losing part of my leg in a couple of months. I am not in Wisconsin but in North Carolina, where you can't make over $500 a month for a family of four to obtain Medicaid. Welcome to America!!

I attended the funeral of a 51-year-old friend last night. Very sad to say the least. He has had heart trouble for the last 12 years. He was a veteran, but worked for companies that didn't provide adequate health insurance. The heart medication he was taking cost over $300 out of pocket per month, so he would cheat and only take half a pill or even skip a day to save money. This may have nothing to do with his sudden death, but it is an example of what not being able to afford prescription medications can possibly do to a younger person. And this is America, the richest nation in the World.

THE CRUNCH IS ON

American workers who are enrolled in employer-provided health coverage paid on average 79 percent more for that coverage in 2003 than they did in 1996, according to the U.S. Agency for Healthcare Research and Quality. The average employee contributed $1,275 for family coverage in 1996, compared with $2,283 for family coverage in 2003. Employers have borne an even greater share of the increasing premiums. The average employer's contribution for a private-sector employee with family coverage increased 89.3 percent—from $3,679 in 1996 to $6,966 in 2003.

More recent survey data from the Kaiser Family Foundation are even more sobering. In 2005, an employer-sponsored family plan cost a total of $10,880—more than the $10,712 that a full-time minimum wage worker makes in a year. On average, the employer picks up $8,167 and the worker $2,713 of the insurance bill. For a single person, the average cost in 2005 was $4,023, with $3,413 paid by the employer and $610 by the employee.

At the same time, according to Kaiser's 2005 Annual Employer Health Benefits Survey, the percentage of businesses offering health insurance to workers has declined steadily over the last five years as the cost of providing coverage has zoomed ahead of inflation and wage growth. Sixty percent of companies offered coverage to workers in 2005, down from 69 percent in 2000. The decline is almost entirely because few small businesses are offering health benefits; 98 percent of businesses with two hundred or more workers offer health coverage. In a statement accompanying the release of the survey, Drew E. Altman, the president of the Kaiser Family Foundation, pointed to the "low-wage workers who are being hurt the most by the steady drip, drip, drip of coverage draining out of the employer-based health insurance system."

The overall average rise in premiums eased off a bit in 2005, to 9.2 percent, compared with 11.2 percent in 2004. The 2005 increase ended four consecutive years of double-digit increases, but the 2005 rate of growth was still more than three times the 2.7 percent increase in worker earnings and two and a half times the inflation rate of 3.5 percent.

The pressure just gets worse. Average individual out-of-pocket expenses—copayments, deductibles, and coinsurance—for workers with insurance climbed from $708 in 2000 to $1,366 in 2005, according to *USA Today*. The sticker shock for these out-of-pocket expenses is likely to worsen as more companies eliminate set copays of $5, $15, and $20 for doctor visits and switch instead to a coinsurance model that requires you to pay 20 to 30 percent of the bill.

INSURED BUT BANKRUPT

If you think the health-care crisis in the United States involves only people without insurance, you should talk to Brenda Surin.

Surin, in her midfifties, lives in Portage, Michigan, near Kalamazoo. She has been divorced for fourteen years and has three grown children. For most of her life, she had sporadic bouts of muscle weakness that her doctors were unable to definitively diagnose. "I learned to ignore the symptoms," she said, "because I kept getting misdiagnosed. I was diagnosed with multiple sclerosis, Parkinson's disease, lupus—all major serious illnesses. I would just rest, tough it out, and keep on pushing. But as I got older, it got more difficult."

During her married years, Surin operated a day-care center in Illinois and hoped at some point to enroll in college, despite her physical problems. In 1989, while in the throes of her divorce, she moved to Michigan to be near her family. She enrolled in a community college and later transferred to Western Michigan University, in Kalamazoo, where she started work on an undergraduate degree. While enrolled at Western, she was covered by student insurance, which she remembers had limited benefits.

Her medical condition worsened. She looked for a doctor who could find a correct diagnosis. She started having vision problems, which were ascribed to migraine headaches. She lost fourteen teeth. At one point she was told that her problems were psychological and she was advised to see a psychiatrist. "The psychiatrist did a work-up and concluded that there was nothing psychologically wrong with me," Surin recalled. "I was described as stable, both emotionally and mentally, and able to cope well with pain."

In 1997, a close friend whose husband is a dentist insisted that Surin take a job in her husband's dental office so she would have access to group insurance. She took the job, despite her increased inability to work, and signed up for the plan with Blue Cross Blue Shield of Michigan. But it was little comfort. "I knew something was terribly wrong . . . and I couldn't get a diagnosis to help me," she said.

Then in 2000, a relatively minor car accident changed her life. She suffered a whiplashlike injury that greatly exacerbated her previous symptoms. Within three months of the accident, she had lost 30 percent of the muscle mass on the left side of her body. She and her friend sought out yet another doctor. Because of the accident, the new doctor ordered an MRI, or magnetic resonance imaging, of Surin's head and back.

The MRI revealed that she was suffering from a rare birth defect called Chiari Malformation, a deformity of the skull that allows part of the brain to protrude into the top of the spinal canal, putting pressure on the brain, brain stem, and spinal column. It is especially difficult to treat in adults.

Surin saw three different neurologists in Michigan. None of them had ever done the surgery suggested by the National Institute of Neu-rological Disorders and Stroke for treatment of adults with Chiari Malformation. Her brother, a registered nurse, went online and found three hospitals in the United States where the surgery could be per-formed. One was nearby: the Mayo Clinic in Rochester, Minnesota. She underwent surgery at the Mayo Clinic in April 2001. Surin's sur-geon had performed sixty such surgeries with a 70 percent success rate. Her surgery was successful. Another woman, however, who had the same surgery at Mayo two weeks later, died.

Surin was in the hospital for eight days after her surgery and then had to undergo extensive physical therapy. Many of her symptoms disappeared, but others—her muscle weakness and pain—will con-tinue for the rest of her life. She must be careful not to strain herself (she is not supposed to lift anything heavier than five pounds) or bump herself too hard. She can drive, but only on a limited basis be-cause she tires easily and can become disoriented. She has regained some of her muscle mass, and her weight is up to 125 pounds; at her lowest point she weighed 87 pounds. She spends three, thirty-minute periods a day in traction.

After the physical suffering and emotional uncertainty of her condition, Surin had yet another assault to overcome, this one man-made: the health-care system. Despite every effort to avoid it, she was forced to declare bankruptcy in November 2004. Even with group health insurance coverage, her surgery and subsequent treat-ment had left her more than $50,000 in debt.

She is not alone. A study by the Commonwealth Fund found that an estimated 77 million people—almost two out of five adults—struggled to pay medical bills in 2003. The majority of people with medical debt problems reported that they had insurance when their difficulties began. In fact, medical bills cause almost half of personal bankruptcies.

In Surin's case, her insurance paid 80 percent of most of her medical bills and 70 percent of the charges for her extensive physical therapy, leaving her with copayments and deductibles in the tens of thousands. Given her physical limitations, she knew there was likely no way she could find a job that would allow her to repay that amount. Friends tried to help her financially. Before her condition had gotten so debilitating, Surin had bred Rhodesian Ridgeback dogs and had served on the board of the Rhodesian Ridgeback Club of the United States. One of her dogs, Zulu, won best of breed in 1996 at the prestigious Westminster dog show in New York. The club rallied behind Surin and raised $7,000 for her medical costs. Despite the help, "I was still overwhelmed by medical bills," she said.

Without insurance, Surin probably would have been eligible for Medicaid, but it might not have helped her. "There was no one in Michigan who could have performed this surgery," she said. "And there was no way Medicaid would have paid for me to go out of state for an operation. For me, Medicaid would have been a death sentence."

In January 2003, Surin applied for Social Security disability. She got it on her second appeal and in May 2005 started receiving $531 a month, based on her work history. A couple of months later, in July, she became eligible for Medicare. She is allowed to earn up to $750 a month while maintaining her disability status, giving her a maximum income on disability of $1,281 a month. She lives with her brother and takes a weekly class in massage therapy. She is unable to attend college but hopes someday to complete the twenty-two credit hours she needs to get her undergraduate degree from Western Michigan University. Her ultimate dream: to become a professor.

"It has been so humiliating and degrading for me," she said. "I've worked all my life. I've always been a go-getter. The hardest part for me, as a strong independent woman, has been holding on to my dignity in the face of all this. The insurance issue was terrible. I kept thinking, what happens to people who don't have insurance, who don't have friends and family? I was blessed, but even with that I had to declare bankruptcy. The system really makes me mad."

A SWAMP OF MEDICAL BILLS

Even if you have insurance, you can be financially swamped by a serious illness or an accident and, like Brenda Surin, find yourself facing personal bankruptcy. But the financial strain does not have to be that acute. A 2005 poll by *USA Today*, the Kaiser Family Foundation, and the Harvard School of Public Health found that more than one in five Americans has an overdue medical bill and nearly 20 percent say health-care costs are their second-biggest monthly expense after housing.

The Commonwealth Fund—which has estimated that 16 million Americans are underinsured, facing the financial strain of medical bills despite having some coverage—released a study in 2005 showing that nearly 71 million working Americans between the ages of nineteen and sixty-four—about 40 percent of the total—reported having problems paying for their medical expenses in 2003. The study also said that 27.7 million working adults carried medical debt in 2003. According to the U.S. Agency for Healthcare Research and Quality, the percentage of Americans under age sixty-five whose family out-of-pocket spending for health care, including insurance, exceeds $2,000 a year rose from 37.3 percent in 1996 to 43.1 percent in 2003.

The Commonwealth Fund also reported that rates of medical-bill stress among the underinsured were roughly equal to those cited by the uninsured: 46 percent of underinsured individuals were contacted by a collection agency regarding their medical bills, compared with 44 percent of uninsured individuals. Moreover, 54 percent of the underinsured report going without needed care, compared with 59 percent of the uninsured. This means they failed to fill a prescription, skipped a test or follow-up, failed to visit a doctor for a medical problem, and/or did not get specialist care.

For a clearer idea of just how disrupting increases in health-care costs can be on household finances for those with insurance, consider a 2005 survey by the Employee Benefit Research Institute. More than a quarter of those surveyed said they had decreased their contributions to a retirement plan because of health costs; 24 percent said they experienced difficulty paying for basic necessities, such as food, heat, and housing. Figure 3 shows a summary of the results, broken down by income.

KNOW WHAT YOUR INSURANCE PROTECTS

As the stories of Brenda Surin and many others illustrate, the financial protection health insurance offers has its limits—especially for a serious medical problem or an accident. This increasingly has become the case as medical costs have skyrocketed ahead of inflation and companies have cut back on coverage, increased employees' premiums, and raised copayments and deductibles. Only 28 percent of employers paid all of their employees' monthly health-care premiums in 2003, down from 35 percent in 1998, according to the U.S. Agency for Healthcare Research and Quality. When illness or accidents strike, they can prove disastrous for lower-income and even average-income workers who may not have a lot of savings to rely on.

Before selecting a policy from an employer menu (or shopping for an individual policy, as we'll discuss in the next chapter), you should be certain you understand the terms used by the health insurance industry. The meanings can vary slightly among insurers, so if a number or explanation doesn't match up with the following definitions, press the insurance provider for more details; there may be costs or exceptions hidden in the differences in jargon.

- *Coinsurance* is the amount you must pay after your health plan's deductible has been met. It's usually expressed as a percentage. For instance, you might have to pay 20 percent of every bill until the total of your own payments hits your *out-of-pocket maximum.*
- *Copayment* is a flat fee you pay for health-care services, regardless of how much the doctor or hospital receives from your insurance

Figure 3

How Americans Cope with Rising Costs

Percentage of individuals with health-care coverage who made each type of shift in resources in 2005 because of health-care cost increases.

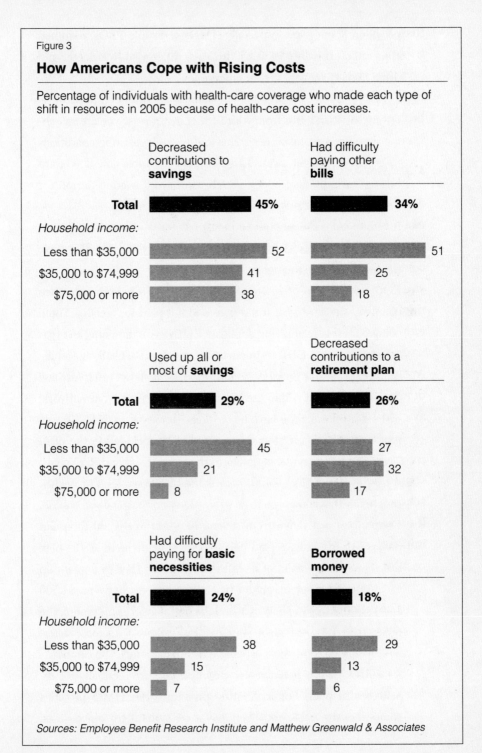

Decreased contributions to **savings**

Total	45%
Household income:	
Less than $35,000	52
$35,000 to $74,999	41
$75,000 or more	38

Had difficulty paying other **bills**

Total	34%
Household income:	
Less than $35,000	51
$35,000 to $74,999	25
$75,000 or more	18

Used up all or most of **savings**

Total	29%
Household income:	
Less than $35,000	45
$35,000 to $74,999	21
$75,000 or more	8

Decreased contributions to a **retirement plan**

Total	26%
Household income:	
Less than $35,000	27
$35,000 to $74,999	32
$75,000 or more	17

Had difficulty paying for **basic necessities**

Total	24%
Household income:	
Less than $35,000	38
$35,000 to $74,999	15
$75,000 or more	7

Borrowed money

Total	18%
Household income:	
Less than $35,000	29
$35,000 to $74,999	13
$75,000 or more	6

Sources: Employee Benefit Research Institute and Matthew Greenwald & Associates

provider. Some plans, especially HMOs and some PPOs, require a copayment, usually $10 to $30 for each office visit to a doctor and often higher copayments for emergency care.

- *Credit for prior coverage* may be something you need to prove—normally with a letter from your former insurer—if you are switching employers or insurance plans and need preexisting conditions to be covered right away. This is especially important if you are buying an individual policy, which can have a waiting period for preexisting conditions.

- A *deductible* is the amount you must pay for your medical bills before your insurance kicks in. Usually the higher the deductible runs, the less expensive the policy is.

- *EOB (explanation of benefits)* is a statement from your insurance company showing what it has paid and not paid for a claim. Some companies resist supplying duplicate EOBs, so maintaining an organized file of your EOBs is important if you need to challenge a bill.

- An *EPO (exclusive provider organization) plan* allows you to use any doctor or hospital within the insurance provider's current network, without a referral. You have no coverage, however, outside the current network even if your doctor used to be included in the plan. There can be copayments similar to those for HMO and PPO plans.

- A *fee-for-service (indemnity) plan* is the traditional kind of health-care policy that allows you to go to any doctor or hospital you choose. Deductibles can range from several hundred to several thousand dollars. After you have paid bills totaling your deductible, the plan usually pays 80 percent of all bills; you pay the other 20 percent up to an out-of-pocket maximum that generally runs between $1,500 and $3,000. After you have reached the out-of-pocket maximum, the policy pays 100 percent of your medical expenses. In most states, fee-for-service is the most expensive health insurance you can buy.

- An *HMO (health maintenance organization)* is essentially a prepaid health plan. For a monthly premium, the HMO provides comprehensive care. You likely pay a copayment for office visits, but most HMO plans have no deductibles. (The exception to the no-deductible rule is an HMO that is eligible for a health savings account.) There are usually no forms to fill out or bills to keep track of. You are, however, quite limited in your choice of doctors, hospitals, and other health-care providers. You commonly must get a referral from your primary-care physician to see a specialist; if you don't, your treatment with the specialist is not covered. Though HMOs were designed to control costs, they have been the source of many consumer complaints. These complaints were often because of coverage limitations or the fact that some doctors were compensated for denying treatment or referrals to patients or punished for providing what was considered by the HMO to be excessive treatment, although both problems have lessened in recent years. Because of their comprehensive, deductible-free coverage, HMOs often compete with the most affordable health insurance options.

- *An HSA (health savings account)* is a less expensive, high-deductible policy linked to a tax-free savings account that can be used to pay medical bills before the policy's deducible is met. (For a more extensive discussion of HSAs, see chapter 4.)

- *Lifetime maximum* is the maximum amount of covered expenses your insurance company will pay in your lifetime. Look for a policy with a lifetime maximum of at least $3 million.

- *Out-of-pocket maximum* is the amount of coinsurance you must pay yourself before an insurance policy will pay 100 percent of your bills. It may or may not include the deductible. The term *stop-loss* is sometimes used to refer to the point at which you have met your deductible and paid your out-of-pocket maximum.

- *A POS (point-of-service) plan* is like a PPO except that you need a referral from your primary-care physician to see an out-of-network doctor, for which you may have to pay extra. Without the referral, you will likely have to pay the entire bill for the out-of-network physician.

- *A PPO (preferred provider organization) plan* is a cross between a fee-for-service plan and an HMO. You can see any doctor you choose without a referral, although if the physician is outside the insurance plan's network you will probably be reimbursed at a lower rate. For network doctors, you usually have only a copayment for office visits. There can be varying copayments—as well as deductibles, coinsurance, and out-of-pocket maximums—depending on the policy. Most plans that are eligible for use with a health savings account are PPOs with a high deductible tacked on.

These terms, of course, aren't exclusive to individual policies. Many employers offer a menu of plans for you to select from that usually includes HMOs, PPOs, and traditional indemnity plans. Increasingly, companies are offering HSAs and dropping indemnity plans because they are so expensive. We'll look at employer-based coverage in chapter 10.

MATCHING POLICIES TO YOUR WALLET

You should try to become as knowledgeable as possible about the health insurance options offered by your employer, or available on the individual market, and pick the best coverage for your personal situation. For instance, if your primary concern is to limit your financial outlays resulting from an illness or accident, there are several guidelines you should follow.

Look for a policy with a low stop-loss. This is the maximum out-of-pocket amount you must pay in a given year in coinsurance and deductibles before your policy starts paying 100 percent of your bills. Coinsurance is the portion of bills you must pay, typically 20 to 30 percent, before the stop-loss kicks in. Stop-loss amounts can vary from as little as $1,200 to many thousands of dollars.

Consider a policy with a high lifetime payment cap. A million dollars, which is the cap on some policies, may sound like a lot of money. At today's exploding medical prices, however, it's possible for a single illness or two to eat that up. Three to five million dollars is a much safer cap.

Get secondary coverage if possible. If both you and your spouse work and both have group health insurance available through your jobs, each can sign up for the insurance and list the other as a dependent. You won't receive double payments for medical bills, but each of you will have secondary coverage that will usually pay the part of a medical bill not paid by the primary insurer. This is known as *coordination of benefits* and usually works only with employer-based group insurance. Such a strategy may cost you more each month in premiums if they are not paid by your respective employers, but can really pay off in the event of illness or an accident.

My wife and I were enrolled in each other's coverage as a secondary policy for years. My medical bills were paid through my insurer, hers by her insurer. Her insurer, as my secondary carrier, paid anything left over in my case; my insurer, as her secondary carrier, paid the balance on her bills. This almost always meant that together the insurers paid 100 percent of our bills after the annual deductibles on the policies had been met. It also meant double the paperwork, but that was a small price to pay. Even if in some years the extra premiums exceed your benefits, the peace of mind may still make it worthwhile; its value can also increase as you get older and, presumably, your medical expenses rise. We have continued this practice through a secondary retiree policy. My wife recently underwent a series of outpatient tests at a Denver hospital that cost $8,427. Our primary insurer paid all but $1,860 of the bill; the balance was paid by our secondary insurance, which runs us $3,400 a year and has a $300 deductible, which she had already met. This means that we each have to have $3,700 a year in bills that are not paid by our primary carrier to break even—not hard to do these days, as the single Denver bill shows.

Double coverage, of course, doesn't work for everyone. It depends on how comprehensive your employer-provided policies are, as well as how much of the premiums you and your spouse are required to pay. It didn't pay for Katy Hope and her husband, Dr. Alexander Cohen, who live in New York City. Both are covered by her health policy at a publisher, where she works as a copywriter. Her coverage through an EPO is quite comprehensive: there is no annual deductible; office copays are $15; emergency room visits are $50; and prescriptions run between $10 and $35, depending on the drug. Her cost is relatively modest at $56.86 every two weeks, or $1,478.36 a year. Cohen, a resident in emergency medicine, could get similar coverage for them through his job, but it would cost $277.23 every two weeks, or $7,207.98 a year. In looking at a recent year of medical expenses, Hope said her insurance has paid about $5,000 toward their bills; their outlay was less than $500. "Double coverage would have hurt, not helped, us financially," she said. In addition, Cohen receives a $1,000 per year benefit payment because he does not accept his employer's coverage. This effectively reduces their annual premium on Hope's employer coverage to $478.36.

Watch out for fine-print limits on certain things like chemotherapy, physical therapy, and home health care, where some insurance companies try to cut corners on coverage.

Avoid policies with payment caps on specific medical and surgical procedures. "Minimed," or limited benefit, plans have set amounts they will pay for things like surgeries and hospital room and board.* These policies are less expensive but could leave you woefully

*Another kind of coverage you might have to be wary of, if some members of Congress have their way, is that allowed by legislation that would permit insurance companies to bypass state health insurance regulations. When this book was going to press, the House was again considering a measure, the Health Care Choice Act, under which insurance companies operating in one state could sell individual health policies to residents of another state even if the policies did not meet the standards of the second state. Unless strong federal regulations

underinsured for a major illness or accident. Also watch out for limitations on regular policies. Some, for instance, will have unrealistically low caps on certain surgeries or medical procedures. One example: a $50,000 limit for organ-transplant surgery. Such surgery can cost four to five times that, or more.

If, on the other hand, you have enough savings to cover more of the expenses of a medical emergency like the one Brenda Surin encountered, you should consider a high-deductible policy, perhaps one linked to a health savings account, or HSA. You might, for example, be less concerned about coverage for things like doctor visits. While you may seem to be paying more on a regular basis, your premiums should be less, and you will be covered for a more serious and costly illness.

THOSE MYSTERIOUS CHARGES

Hospital care accounts for about one-third of health-care spending, which totaled about $6,423 per person in 2005, according to *USA Today*.

Most of us have never seen a hospital bill—at least not the full itemized one that goes to our insurance companies or Medicare. We get an explanation of benefits (EOB), showing what our insurer paid a hospital on our behalf. Then, perhaps, we get a bill for charges that the insurer did not pay. If there is a patient bill, it is usually not very long—one or two pages—with the amounts due listed and very little explanation or detail. Hospital charges and billing are processes over which we have almost no control. Patients with good insurance have

---

are enacted, which is considered unlikely, such policies, with skeletal benefits, could leave many people massively underinsured. Critics call them "low-premium junk policies." Already passed by the House and initially rejected by the Senate but still under consideration by that body is another bill creating so-called associated health plans, which would allow small businesses to offer health plans that could also bypass state regulations. Yet another Senate bill would extend associated health plans to anyone, much like the House bill.

little incentive to think much about the issue. I have heard people brag that they have never seen a bill from a hospital. That may change as more and more medical costs get shifted to the consumer.

Insurance companies often have contracts with hospitals that they will accept the insurance payment as payment in full and not bill the patient. One of the many irrational aspects of our health-care system is that hospitals usually charge uninsured patients—and insured patients whose insurance benefits have run out—more, often much more, than patients with insurance. That's because insurance companies have agreements with hospitals for special rates. Think about it for a minute. If a person pays cash for a hospital bill, the chances are he or she will pay much more than an insured patient whose insurance company may take weeks or months to pay the bill. If someone cannot or does not pay the bill, the hospital can take him or her to court and seize assets, including a home.

Hospital charges for uninsured patients can vary from hospital to hospital. So can the aggressiveness with which a hospital attempts to collect bills. In the face of complaints, bad publicity, and lawsuits over what some call gouging, a number of hospitals have started giving uninsured patients a discount off the "sticker price," sometimes the same break given to insurance companies or Medicare. Others refuse to budge.

This two-tier system doesn't just involve the uninsured. An online news service, NorthJersey.com, in 2005 reported the story of a retired New Jersey butcher, physically and mentally devastated from a series of strokes, who was sued by his hospital for $160,170.35. He was covered by his private insurance for the first twenty-one days in the hospital. After that, he was on his own and no longer getting discounted prices. His hospital stay lasted thirty-eight days. The $160,170.35 was only for the days not covered by insurance. Starting on day twenty-two, he was charged much more—sometimes as much as ten times more—than what his insurer would have been charged for the same services during his first twenty-one days. This conclusion was based on what Medicare would have paid. (Although he wasn't on Medicare, many insurance companies use it as a benchmark when setting their payments, which generally run a bit more than Medicare's. The problem is that Medicare's payment rates are very complex—some charges are bundled with others—and are generally unavailable to the public. NorthJersey.com was able to calculate what the Medicare payments would have been only with the help of the Health Care Payers Coalition of New Jersey, a nonprofit alliance of benefit plans.) One example: He was charged $1,025 for monitoring his cardiac function; Medicare, and presumably his insurance company, would have paid $96.50 for the same service, according to NorthJersey.com. NorthJersey.com reported that had the man been discharged on day twenty-one of his stay, the hospital would have accepted his insurer's check for $46,865 as payment in full for all the services he received. For the seventeen additional days, he would have been charged only about $50,000—instead of $160,170.35—had he been given the same discounts as his health plan got for the first twenty-one days. The man's relatives tried to get the hospital to accept a lower price, in line with the insurer's discounts. The hospital refused, demanding full price. New Jersey hospitals, by the way, have some of the highest hospital "sticker price" markups in the nation, almost four and a half times higher than costs. The national average is a bit under two and a half times costs, according to the Institute for Health and Socioeconomic Policy (IHSP), which is the research arm of the California nurses' union.

Some other data from the IHSP help explain why health costs are so high in America.

- The world's thirteen-largest drug companies posted $62 billion in profits for 2004.
- U.S. hospitals reached aggregate profits of $26.3 billion in 2004.
- The twenty-largest HMOs in the United States had profits of $10.8 billion for their latest posted fiscal year in 2004.

- Twelve top HMO executives earned $222.6 million in direct compensation in the latest fiscal year. The top twelve drug company executives made $192.7 million in the same period.
- Corporate mergers in the health-care industry have consumed $1.5 trillion in the last dozen years.

"These numbers should be a wake-up call to the American public," said Deborah Burger, president of the California Nurses Association, in a statement to the press. "At a time when nearly 46 million Americans have no health coverage, medical bills cause half of all bankruptcies, and insecurity characterizes how tens of millions of others view the health safety net for their families, we have a national scandal. Wall Street promised Americans that market domination of health care would produce improved quality, increased access, lower costs, and expanded choice. It has failed spectacularly on all counts."

NEGOTIATING IS POSSIBLE

Advocates of consumer-directed health care argue that people should shop around for the best medical prices. That's virtually impossible with hospitals because their prices vary depending not only on your insurance carrier, or whether you have insurance, but also on how hospitals compute costs and expenses. This, in turn, can be affected by how often doctors order unnecessary tests, the number of complicated cases, and the number of uninsured patients that are treated. (Hospitals, by law, must treat anyone who comes to an emergency room, regardless of ability to pay.)*

---

*Which patients actually get billed depends on a hospital's policy. Despite the federal law, it is not uncommon for hospitals to turn away uninsured ER patients during overcrowded periods or to transfer them to other hospitals. Sometimes specialists refuse to come to an ER in the middle of the night to treat uninsured patients. Delays often result. Hospitals that engage in so-called patient dumping, however, risk being dropped from the Medicare program.

You are unlikely to be privy to much of that information. Basically, there are no set prices. Hospitals do have what is called a charge master, a list of "sticker prices" for thousands of items and procedures, but it has little to do with real charges or negotiated prices paid by Medicare, Medicaid, and insurance companies. The *Milwaukee Journal Sentinel* reported in December 2005 that the charge master price of an appendectomy in Wisconsin ranged from $4,751 to $12,450, depending on the hospital. The governor of West Virginia, Joe Manchin, told the Associated Press that same month that he had no idea how much his hernia surgery cost. He had received bills for months and then was sent a refund for an overpayment—even though he paid the amount he was billed. Manchin is calling for a state law that would require simplified and transparent billing. The California HealthCare Foundation, in a 2005 study, had people pose as patients seeking pricing information on elective procedures at sixty-four hospitals in the state. It turned out that obtaining a price depended on luck and persistence. While 76 percent of the inquiries were eventually answered with a firm or an estimated price, more than a third of the callers had to make three or more calls to get an answer. One caller to one hospital had to talk to seventeen different people to get an answer. Some hospitals would give only a range of prices, not an exact figure.

You can often get a glimpse into this world of idiosyncratic pricing by looking at the explanation of benefits, or EOB, that your insurance company sends to inform you of what it paid and thus, also, what you owe. I recently received an EOB from my insurer showing hospital charges totaling $30,663.13 that stretched the definition of *explanation.* The charges were itemized by date and amounts, but there was no further information. I had no idea what the $510 charge on one date was for, nor did I know what three separate $13 charges could represent. On some charges there was a coinsurance payment due from me. On other charges there was no coinsurance and a notation: "Our contracting provider has agreed to accept our payment allowance and should not bill the patient for the provider write-off. Refer to the allowable charge section of the patient's contract." For example, the insurer paid $282.83 toward the mysterious $510 charge, and the hospital agreed to write off, or cancel, the remaining $227.17. It got even stranger on a charge of $273 for another unidentified medical moment. The insurer paid $30.11, the hospital canceled $229.99, and I owed a coinsurance payment of $12.90. That means for a charge of $273, the hospital agreed to accept $43.01. It's a good thing these people aren't trying to earn a living selling cars.

The bottom line: For its charge of $30,663.13, the hospital actually was paid $4,064.99 by my insurance company, and I paid coinsurance of $807.70 (which was paid not by me but by my secondary insurance company), bringing the total to $4,872.69. The hospital wrote off $16,137.61 and was still sorting out $9,652.83 when it sent the EOB. With the insurance contract, my hospital will eventually be paid around $7,000 for a bill that began life at more than $30,000. Someone without any insurance would be facing the prospect of having to pay the full bill of $30,663.13.

This hospital bill illustrates the value of being covered by a secondary health insurance policy. As mentioned earlier, of course, you need to weigh the cost of secondary coverage against the benefits you might collect. While it's impossible to predict the future, your past health record should have some bearing on the matter.

If you are faced with significant hospital bills because you are uninsured or underinsured for a procedure, you should try to bargain hard with the hospital to get a discount. You may not get as much of a discount as a big insurance company, but many hospitals—unlike the one that treated the New Jersey butcher—are often willing to negotiate a lower price and even work out a payment arrangement. Some hospitals, however, won't do both. If they lower the price, they want to be paid all at once. Of course, what they want and what they can actually get may be quite different. Be prepared to play hardball. Do the following:

Keep a log while you are in the hospital of the services you get and when you get them. This log will help you review your bill; the vast majority of hospital bills that are reviewed are found to contain errors that result in a reduction of charges. (Chapter 7 covers medical logs in more detail.)

Demand an itemized hospital bill and compare it with your log. If you don't remember a test or procedure, or have no record of it on your logs, ask for paperwork on it, including the results.

Ask the hospital for a discount that would reduce your bill so it would be in line with what Medicare or an insurance company pays. As the case of the New Jersey butcher and my EOB showed, that could reduce your bill by as much as two-thirds, or more. The problem is finding out what Medicare or an insurance company would have paid. Larry Levitt, a vice president of the Kaiser Family Foundation, said hospital billing is so complex that there is no realistic way for the average consumer to ferret out this information. Based on news reports, my advice is to assume the insurance or Medicare discount is 50 percent and try to negotiate to at least that point. Ask hospital officials to tell you what an insurer they do business with would have paid for your bill. Remember, hospitals are constantly being accused of gouging patients and are under increasing pressure to accept a negotiated payment. There are lawsuits challenging their billing methods, and some states are pursuing legislation that would address the unfairness in the system. Don't forget that hospital profit margins hit an all-time high in 2004, the latest year for which data are available, according to the American Hospital Association. Taking you to court for the full "sticker price" of a bill may not be a hospital's best public relations option.

You can usually negotiate a lower hospital or medical bill—and you should try. Unfortunately, according to a 2005 survey by *USA Today*, the Kaiser Family Foundation, and the Harvard School of

Public Health, few people see alternatives to lowering their health-care bills beyond skipping care:

- Only about 11 percent of adults reported negotiating with a physician, hospital, or other provider to get a lower price for health-care services. That figure jumped to 24 percent for the uninsured, compared with just 8 percent for those with insurance.
- The results of negotiating were mixed, but 58 percent of those who did try to negotiate reported they got a lower price.
- Only 9 percent said they went to the Internet to find lower prices for prescription drugs; an anemic 6 percent reported going to the Internet to price other health-care services.
- Just 7 percent of insured adults reported that they switched doctors to lower their out-of-pocket expenses.
- About a third (35 percent) said their doctor had never explained the costs associated with a recommended procedure; 17 percent said this had rarely happened.

Those are bleak numbers, but the good news out of this survey is that there is room to negotiate; don't assume that you have to accept the bloated prices on your bills. Just consider that you're going to win a better price for health care at least six out of ten times.

Consider hiring a lawyer as a last resort. If you have a big hospital bill and the hospital won't budge, you have a lot at risk, especially if you own a home or other assets.

A COSTLY ASSUMPTION

When George Dennis, a civil engineer in Richmond, Virginia, changed jobs in November 2004, he asked if his wife, Nancy, would be included under the health benefits at his new company. The answer was yes. He checked no further, assuming this meant that the company would pay her premiums, as was the case with his former employer.

He was in for a rude surprise.

George, who was then fifty-eight, found out that while his wife would indeed have access to the company's group plan through United Healthcare, the couple would be responsible for paying 100 percent of her premiums. Most of his premiums, but his alone, would be company-paid. In addition, the new insurance turned out to be less comprehensive than their previous coverage. Because Nancy, then sixty, suffers from a chronic illness and requires expensive care, the couple suddenly faced significant extra outlays—almost $12,000 a year for premiums and medical expenses. George's salary at his new company—which has only nineteen employees and is much smaller than his previous company—was about the same as at his previous job, so there was no cushion to help offset the added expenses.

"My husband just assumed I would be covered, which was a logical assumption," Nancy said.

Their previous employer-provided coverage had cost about $80 a month for both of them; the new coverage runs $380.29 for each two-week pay period, and all but $54.41 of that is for Nancy's coverage. That's a premium jump of $8,955 a year. In addition, Nancy estimates they spend at least another $3,000 a year for medical expenses that were included in the previous plan but are not covered under the new policy.

George and Nancy Dennis have no choice but to pay the extra premiums and expenses. It's the only way Nancy can get coverage. "My medical problem is a constant-care problem," she said. "It's not as though I can go for a year without care. If we leave a group, my preexisting conditions might not be covered for a year, if then. So it's the only realistic way I can get health insurance." Not surprisingly, she has also been turned down for long-term-care insurance, which might have covered some of the extra medical expenses they are paying out of pocket.

Nancy's problems began in 1990 in California when she had a sudden acceleration of muscle weakness and other symptoms that caused her to go into respiratory failure and cardiac arrest. She was diagnosed with Guillain-Barré syndrome, a rare disorder in which the body's immune system attacks parts of the nervous system, leading to partial paralysis. According to the Web site of the National Institute of Neurological Disorders and Strokes, most patients eventually recover from Guillain-Barré syndrome, but there is no cure and some individuals continue to have varying degrees of weakness. Nancy recovered somewhat from her 1990 attack but still has residual muscle weakness and requires a mechanical ventilator to breathe through a tracheotomy tube in her throat. She uses a $22,000 motorized wheelchair—for which she and her husband had to pay most of the price tag—to get around. She also must wear a urinary catheter.

Although disabled, Nancy—who calls her computer, with its Internet connection and e-mail, a "lifeline"—said she had not worked enough continuous quarters prior to her illness to qualify for Social Security disability, which would make her eligible for Medicare even though she is not yet sixty-five. A nurse by training, she had worked as a medical claims adjuster for several insurers before she got sick.

She is quick to assert that her previous health-care plan, a preferred provider organization, or PPO—which allowed out-of-network care but paid for it at a lower rate—was not without its faults and problems. She says, however, that her new plan, also a PPO, covers less than her old plan and has proved more difficult in terms of filing claims and getting approvals for services. She is allowed sixty home health-care visits a year; her tracheotomy tube must be replaced every three months, her urinary catheter every three to four weeks. In addition, because she is not mobile, her heart, blood pressure, and lungs must be monitored. The maximum annual allowance for durable medical equipment like her ventilator and wheelchair is $2,500. Her tracheotomy tube replacement alone costs $400, or $1,600 a year. Plus she must pay a maintenance fee of $131 a month for her ventilator. She is also equipped with a generator and a backup battery in case of a power failure. "I'm very frugal," she said. "I try to use equipment over and over. Otherwise, we would use up our allowance in a couple of months. I try to save the allowance for absolute necessities."

She complained about not having a specific health-care coordinator assigned to her case, which meant she constantly had to deal with different people who often had limited knowledge about her situation. One result was that claims sometimes were rejected the first time around. In November 2005, however, she was able to get United Healthcare to assign her a specific coordinator, which has helped speed processing of her medical claims. Still, claims occasionally get rejected. "But I don't give up," she said. "I'm a fighter. I won't take no for an answer. I'm an insurance company's worst nightmare."

3

Off the Job

I left a job that had health insurance because I thought I was insurable.

—HENRY HAMMAN

America has always prided itself on being a land of opportunity. The health-care crisis is putting that in jeopardy. Full annual premiums for employer-provided family coverage soared 9.2 percent to almost $11,000 in 2005. As a result, many employers are scaling back coverage. Like pensions, employer-sponsored health plans are shrinking, shifting more costs to employees, or disappearing altogether. In 2003, 60.4 percent of Americans had health coverage through their jobs; that dropped to 59.8 percent in 2004 and is widely expected to fall below 50 percent by the end of the decade. Our system of employer-based health insurance, in place since World War II, is crumbling, with nothing in the wings to replace it—a fact that is not lost on workers. In a study released in June 2005 by the Employee Benefit Research Institute, 75 percent of workers surveyed rated health insurance as either the most important or second-most important job-related benefit (figure 4). The survey included those who had coverage through a spouse's job, which might explain why a

Figure 4

How Workers Rank Employment Benefits

Percentage of workers surveyed.

	Most Important	Second-most Important
Health insurance	**60%**	15%
Retirement savings plan	17	**38**
Paid time off	5	11
Retiree health insurance	5	9
Pension plan	4	9
Long-term care insurance	3	6
Life insurance	3	4
Disability insurance	1	6
Stock options	–	1
Others	1	1

A dash indicates fewer than 0.5 percent.

Source: Employee Benefit Research Institute, 2004

full 75 percent—the level of support among Americans for guaranteed health coverage—did not rank it first.

A lot of would-be entrepreneurs are having second thoughts about leaving their jobs because of the burden of health insurance. Coverage shock also confronts workers who would like to retire before they are age sixty-five, when they become eligible for Medicare, but whose employers provide no retiree health benefits. These two groups are not mutually exclusive, of course; many people want to retire early in order to start their own businesses. Nowhere is this more obvious than in the large numbers of baby boomers who want to retire early but continue to work on their own terms. Many are blocked only by the lack of health coverage. Those without retiree health benefits, however, are still far better off than those whose employers provide no health insurance whatever. They are forced to purchase individual coverage—if they can afford it and qualify for it. Chapter 5 looks at individual insurance in detail.

The "job lock" linked to an absence of health benefits for those who want to retire before age sixty-five can hurt the economy in two ways. First, it slows the creation of new small-business start-ups and jobs. Overall, small businesses are historically credited with creating as many as 75 percent of all new jobs. Second, it can create job grid-lock as workers, especially those in their fifties and early sixties who might otherwise move on, stay at their jobs simply for the health coverage. This ripples down the line to younger workers trying to move up as well as new job applicants looking for openings.

COBRA AND HIPAA

Those who decide to take the entrepreneurial leap face not only the expense of their coverage but also the strong possibility that they may not be able to purchase individual insurance policies because of preexisting medical conditions. If the company you are leaving has more than twenty employees, a federal law allows you to continue your employer-provided coverage temporarily, but at your expense, under a program known as COBRA, or the Consolidated Omnibus Budget Reconciliation Act. Another federal law also gives you a guar-antee of switching from COBRA to an individual insurance plan later. If your company is too small to be covered by COBRA, you are on your own in the individual insurance market, whose rules depend on the state in which you live. Because it's essentially employer-sponsored group health insurance, COBRA coverage is usually more generous than individual plans.

The details: COBRA allows you and your spouse and eligible chil-dren to continue your employee health insurance benefits for eigh-teen months after you leave your job. You are guaranteed the coverage regardless of preexisting conditions and with no waiting periods. If you qualify for Medicare when you leave your job but your spouse does not, he or she can continue coverage with your employee health insurance for up to thirty-six months. Your spouse is also eligible for thirty-six months of coverage if you die or divorce. You and your spouse are eligible for COBRA even if you have been laid off or fired for any reason other than gross misconduct. There are two hitches to enrolling: You must apply within sixty days and you cannot combine COBRA with any other comprehensive health insurance. One great thing about COBRA is that you are guaranteed the coverage, just as though you were working, in any state that is within your plan's coverage area, not just the state in which you were employed. If you are in an employer-sponsored HMO, however, that coverage area might be quite limited. If you plan to move out of the area and your HMO doesn't offer coverage in your new home, you should consider switching to possibly more expensive traditional coverage during your company's open-enrollment period if feasible. Otherwise, you could wind up with a COBRA policy that covers only emergency services, forcing you to travel to your previous area for other medical care like doctor visits, checkups, and surgery.

The problem with COBRA is that it's expensive. Family coverage can run well over $1,000 a month. The reason it's expensive is that your company is no longer picking up part of the tab; in fact, you can be charged an extra 2 percent on the full premium (what your employer paid plus what you contributed) as an administrative fee.

Because employers must cover all employees, regardless of their health, the group usually includes a mix of risk levels. People with no health problems may find it cheaper to go for an individual policy, especially one with a high deductible that is linked to a health savings account, as discussed in chapters 4 and 5.

Even after your COBRA coverage period expires, it offers you a path to securing guaranteed insurance until you become eligible for Medicare. That's because once you exhaust COBRA, you fall under another federal law: HIPAA, or the Health Insurance Portability and

Accountability Act of 1996. Generally, insurers operating in a state must offer the state's residents two HIPAA-eligible plans that are modeled on their two most popular individual nongroup policies. HIPAA does not, however, regulate rates, which can make HIPAA plans more expensive since insurers must accept all qualified applicants, regardless of their health. But, like COBRA, you are guaranteed the coverage regardless of preexisting conditions and with no waiting periods. Important: You must apply for HIPAA coverage within sixty-three days of exhausting COBRA coverage, or you lose the right to do so.

COBRA and HIPAA can be your route to uninterrupted, albeit expensive, comprehensive coverage until you are eligible for Medicare, especially if you or someone in your family has health problems that may be a barrier to an individual policy. But because the cost of these plans can be high, healthy individuals and families may be better off passing on COBRA in favor of an individual policy. Even if your premiums are increased down the road, it's likely they will still be less than your COBRA payments. But remember, if you forgo COBRA, you cannot qualify for a HIPAA plan later. You can choose only one path.

THE COBRA WINDOW

Henry Hamman's experience is a case study in how you need to weigh the costs of your two options—to COBRA or not to COBRA—when you leave the cozy world of employer-based coverage and strike out on your own.

He and his wife, Kathy—both fifty-nine—left their jobs in Miami in February 2005 to move to Sewanee, Tennessee, where Henry had gone to boarding school. He wanted to start a business there, and they were seeking a less stressful lifestyle.

In Miami, Henry—who holds a Ph.D. in international relations—had been a teacher and administrator at the University of Miami and a partner in a small consulting firm. In addition, he works as a free-lance news correspondent for the *Financial Times* of London. Kathy works as a freelance book editor. Henry planned to continue his consulting and reporting work in Tennessee, as Kathy would continue her editing. There was only one problem: Their health insurance was dependent on Henry's job at the University of Miami.

They had selected a policy with a high annual deductible—$3,000—because the employee portion of the premium was less expensive and they were in good health. When they looked at COBRA prices for their coverage, they decided to buy individual health insurance in Tennessee. It would be cheaper than COBRA, and they would not face another coverage decision when COBRA cut them off in eighteen months.

Before leaving Florida, they filed an application for their policy with Blue Cross Blue Shield of Tennessee. Soon after arriving there, Henry and Kathy contacted an insurance agency to help them with other insurance matters. One of the agents took over their application for health coverage. He recommended they apply for a health savings account with a high deductible and lower premium, exactly what they were looking for. "We wanted a relatively high deductible," Henry said. Then it was just a matter of filing the paperwork. "Blue Cross requested our medical records, which we supplied," Henry recalled. "The agent suggested that we might get 'up-rated' for some relatively minor preexisting conditions. We were fully expecting to pay as much as five hundred dollars a month."

A few days later the agent called. Blue Cross Blue Shield had turned down both Henry and Kathy for any kind of health coverage.

"I was stunned and flabbergasted," Henry remembered. "We were both stunned. I have only been in the hospital overnight once in my entire life—and that was for elective surgery. Kathy has been in the hospital once for an elective procedure and another time when she was eleven years old to have her appendix removed. We are both runners. When Kathy had a stress test a few years ago, she was told she was in the best shape of anybody they had ever seen for her age, in terms of cardiovascular health. We also ride bikes and maintain an active lifestyle. My body mass index is right where it's supposed to be.

"By normal standards I look like a very healthy guy," Henry said. Over the years he occasionally dealt with "slightly elevated cholesterol." In addition, he was under pressure in the months before the move to Tennessee. "Before we left Miami I had been under a lot of stress taking care of my dying mother and later a business partner," Henry explained. "I was close to him; he had been my mentor when I was in graduate school. So I had to deal with two dying people, one after the other. Plus, there were some other stressful work-related situations. So in addition to the slightly elevated cholesterol, I sometimes had trouble sleeping because of anxiety."

Henry's doctor in Miami had prescribed Zocor, a cholesterol-lowering drug, and Xanax, a tranquilizer, to address these two issues. But by the time they moved to Tennessee, Henry was off both medications. "I had to quit taking the Zocor because it was apparently making my hands shake, which is a possible side effect," he said. "At the same time, however, we also moved away from a lot of the stress, which could have also caused my hands to shake. Anyway, the shaking stopped, and I quit taking Zocor and Xanax."

But it was enough to cause a problem with Blue Cross Blue Shield. Getting rejected by one insurer, of course, can make it harder to get accepted by another.

"So Blue Cross had records showing that I had taken Xanax, but it appears it was not clear to them that I had stopped taking it a while ago," Henry said. "Doctors' records are sometimes not very clear. Blue Cross said they were not going to let me have health insurance because I was taking Xanax, which I wasn't. They also said I had 'uncontrolled cholesterol' because the doctor had noted that I had stopped taking the cholesterol medicine."

When it came to Kathy, Blue Cross Blue Shield denied coverage "because of slightly elevated blood pressure, which is easily controlled by inexpensive medication," Henry noted, adding that "she had also been on a low dose of Zocor because of slightly elevated cholesterol." For seemingly minor reasons they were now faced with the prospect that they would be unable to get coverage because of preexisting conditions.

Luckily, the Hammans were still within their sixty-day eligibility window for COBRA. Their insurance agent recommended they sign up, and they did. Their premium to continue their University of Miami coverage came in at $833 a month. Their agent recommended they wait twelve months and then try to get the Blue Cross Blue Shield rejections reversed. Of course, when their COBRA coverage expires in eighteen months, they become eligible for HIPAA coverage, but that coverage will be more expensive than the regular individual coverage they are trying to get through Blue Cross Blue Shield.

In retrospect, their decision to choose a low-premium, high-deductible policy at the University of Miami turned out to be very wise. The Hammans' COBRA coverage, at $833 a month, is the exact policy they had selected before leaving Miami. The difference is that their employer is no longer paying most of the premiums. "It's a good thing that I selected that high-deductible policy at the university," Henry said. "If I had selected regular insurance, the COBRA rate would have been so high we couldn't have afforded it, and we would have had no insurance." Of course, the portability of the coverage is a benefit and an expense. As Henry explained, "We're paying Miami prices for medical coverage in Tennessee, where health care is cheaper." Health insurance has become the couple's single biggest expense in Tennessee, more than their rent on a four-bedroom, two-bath house on an acre of land, and the added expense has slowed Henry's efforts to start a business.

Henry said that he and Kathy were doing "everything they could" to make sure that they would qualify for individual policies with

Blue Cross Blue Shield and not be forced to fall back on a HIPAA plan. "We would have been a hell of a lot better off if we hadn't taken good care of our health for the last five years," he said. "Then we wouldn't have had medical records. Our agent told us that Blue Cross only wants people who don't have anything wrong with them. They're trying to cut their risk pool down to people they never have to pay anything on." He called this a perversion of the idea of insurance. "I left a job that had health insurance because I thought I was insurable," he continued. "But if I'm not insurable, nobody in my age group is."

Henry's experience has solidified his opposition to employer-based health coverage. "We have changed from a country in which an individual had some standing to a country in which your standing is tied to your place in the corporate structure," he said. "We have become a corporate society. The way we provide insurance couldn't be better designed to keep people as wage slaves, to keep them under the thumb of management—because their health insurance is tied to their jobs. I am prepared to vote for practically anyone who wants to do something about the health insurance problem, and I'm prepared to vote against anyone who tells me that the way things are is a good thing."

AGE MATTERS

One of the by-products of the health insurance mess is that older workers who lose their jobs and their coverage usually have a much harder time buying individual policies than younger workers. According to an estimate by the U.S. Agency for Healthcare Research and Quality, one in four Americans between the ages of fifty-one and fifty-seven will be uninsured at some point during the years preceding eligibility for Medicare. The Commonwealth Fund estimates that 20 percent of people between fifty and sixty-four—a total of 7 million people—are uninsured or will be uninsured for a time.

In addition, many workers between the ages of fifty and sixty-four who have put in the necessary years and want to retire early find themselves unable to do so because their employers don't offer retiree health benefits. Only about a third of employers offer such benefits, and their ranks are fading fast. Those workers with job-related coverage but no retiree benefits can, of course, take advantage of COBRA and HIPAA to extend their coverage, but that's an expensive option.

It's unfortunate that older Americans are among the least likely to qualify for less-expensive individual health-care policies. First, these individuals are at a time in their lives when health issues are more likely to develop. Second, because older people are more likely to have a savings cushion, they are good candidates for high-deductible plans with lower premiums, such as health savings accounts. This option is often unavailable to many of them, however, because of insurers' limitations on preexisting conditions.

One bright spot in this otherwise gloomy picture is that 76 million baby boomers are beginning to occupy the fifty to sixty-four age slot, which the *Wall Street Journal* dubs "near elderly." Boomers, unused to sacrifices and very used to having their way, may be inclined to use their political power to force changes in the health-care system for their benefit, such as the new Medicare prescription drug benefit.

The further effects of boomers on the health-care system remain to be seen. But because of a health-care twist back in 1989 that I call the Dan Rostenkowski factor, politicians are paying close attention to this aging generation. In the summer of 1989, Rostenkowski, then a congressman from Illinois and the powerful chairman of the House Ways and Means Committee, was besieged by a crowd of fifty senior citizens in Chicago. According to the *Chicago Tribune*, the protesters—shouting "coward," "recall," and "impeach"—forced him to sprint through a gas station to his car, where minutes earlier an elderly demonstrator had been sprawled across the hood.

The protesters were angry over a new law that provided catastrophic coverage for Medicare recipients, but with an income-tax
surcharge of up to $800 a year that was set to rise to $1,050 in 1993.
That law was soon repealed. The television images of Rostenkowski
under assault by seniors struck fear into the hearts of politicians that
remains to this day. Few want to be pitted against older people on
issues involving medical care and Medicare. According to Henry
Aaron, a health analyst at the Brookings Institution, "Politicians
were traumatized by the Rostenkowski episode, and they remain
traumatized."

4

Health Savings Accounts

One way to help control costs is to interject market forces, and one way to do that is through health savings accounts.

—PRESIDENT GEORGE W. BUSH

Health savings accounts, or HSAs, are the most visible result of a push by the Bush White House and the Republican Congress toward consumer-directed, or consumer-driven, health care, aimed at helping companies lower the costs of providing employee health coverage and helping individuals who must buy their own insurance. As discussed in chapter 1, HSAs were created with little notice in late 2003, when Congress approved a limited prescription drug benefit for Medicare beneficiaries, and became legally available on January 1, 2004. Although HSAs don't solve the big problems facing the health-care system, they do have the potential to make health insurance less expensive for some people.

HSAs are a somewhat strained application of the economic theory of *moral hazard* to the health-care system. Moral hazard is the notion that having insurance will change your behavior in negative ways. The theory holds, for instance, that if your car and house were fully insured, with no deductibles, you would more likely become a careless driver or fail to take the expected precautions to protect your home from a fire or other damage. Apply this concept to health insurance, as many conservative politicians do, and the result is the belief that people with comprehensive coverage, who have to spend relatively little of their own money, will be excessive in their use of health care and become overconsumers; those who have to spend their own money will be cautious, compare prices, and become more efficient health-care consumers. In other words, high deductibles encourage patients to bargain-hunt for their medical care. Thus health savings accounts offer high-deductible policies that shift costs and responsibility as well as choices to individuals. (Moral hazard is also the reason that the new Medicare prescription drug law prohibits participants from buying policies that would cover the gaps in the Medicare drug coverage.) An October 2005 article by Robert Pear in the *New York Times* about proposed cuts in Medicare and Medicaid coverage contained two opposing quotes that nicely summed up the sharp divisions over moral hazard. Representative Nathan Deal, Republican of Georgia, said, "If people have a personal stake in the cost of their health care, they will use it more responsibly." Representative Tammy Baldwin, Democrat of Wisconsin, replied: "Higher co-payments will lead people to forgo needed medical care. To listen to some of the personal responsibility arguments, one might think that people line up to see their doctors the way they line up to see a rock concert or sporting event, and the only way to control this irrational hunger or thirst for medical care is to make it more expensive. I just don't buy that."

Health savings accounts are born of a conviction that market forces will trigger improved health care and lower prices as patients, forced to spend their own money, negotiate for the best deal and use the health-care system sparingly. The problem with this argument is that buying health care is not like buying a car or a refrigerator. Prices are not posted, and doctors rarely discuss their charges; mere mortals cannot hope to comprehend the dizzying and inconsistent list of hospital charges. As Joseph Antos, a scholar at the American Enterprise Institute and formerly assistant director for health and human resources at the Congressional Budget Office, told the *Wall Street Journal* in 2005, "At present, it is nearly impossible to find out in advance what a health service will cost or to compare that cost among health plans or providers." (Advocates of HSAs and consumer-driven health care, of course, argue that if HSAs become the way most people get health care, the medical pricing system will be forced to become more transparent.) A study by the Employee Benefit Research Institute found that while 70 percent of those in consumer-driven health plans like HSAs consider costs when deciding to seek medical care (compared with 40 percent in traditional plans), only 12 percent said they had access to the information they needed to help them compare doctor and hospital costs.

In addition, good nonfinancial information on health care is not that easy to find or always that clear-cut, and most of us simply don't have the expertise to know the kind or level of medical care we require. What if a hospital has a high surgical mortality rate? Does that mean it is substandard and should be avoided? Or does it mean it takes on a lot of difficult and complicated cases?

While the moral hazard theory may be somewhat convincing for certain elective procedures like cosmetic surgery, someone being wheeled into an emergency room in the midst of a heart attack or a stroke is in no position to bargain financially or otherwise over his or her care.

HOW HSAs WORK

A health savings account must be established in conjunction with the purchase of a catastrophic health insurance policy, which, because of its high deductible, is cheaper than traditional coverage. Money you put in an HSA each year is tax free and can be used for payment of health insurance deductibles. You may not, however, use the money to pay the health policy premiums. If you use the money you contribute to the plan, or any of the investment income the money earns, for anything but medical expenses, you must pay taxes and a 10 percent penalty on the amount withdrawn. The account balance can build year to year. When you are sixty-five and eligible for Medicare, you can use the HSA funds for anything you want; if, at that point, you spend the money on nonmedical expenses, however, you must pay taxes on it (but no penalty). If you spend it on medical expenses, the money remains free from federal taxes. The funds are also free from state taxes in most states. Of the forty-one states that have an income tax, as of this writing there are seven that tax contributions to HSAs: Alabama, California, Maine, Massachusetts, New Jersey, Pennsylvania, and Wisconsin.

For individuals, insurance plans must have an annual deductible of $1,050 or more to be eligible for a companion health savings account; for families, the deductible must be $2,100 or more. Individuals can make a contribution to their HSA in any amount up to the insurance plan's deductible but not more than $2,700 a year; families can put in up to $5,450 a year. Both of these limits are inflation-indexed and will increase. If you are over fifty-five when you establish an HSA, you can make an additional catch-up contribution of $700 each year. If your insurance has a higher deductible than the annual limit, the difference is your responsibility. The yearly inflation-indexed out-of-pocket maximum, however, is $5,250 for an individual and $10,500 for a family, regardless of your catastrophic plan; these maximums include deductibles and any copayments or coinsurance you must pay. Remember, too, that because it is invested, an HSA's value can build year to year—or decline in value—depending on how risky the investments are.

"Ideally, the deductible on your policy would match the maximum on your HSA, but there could be a gap if you picked a higher-deductible policy," said Robert Hurley, the chief operating officer for Health Savings Account Solutions at the big online health insurance broker eHealthInsurance (www.ehealthinsurance.com), which is aggressively pushing individual HSA-eligible policies. "But as the account builds year to year, that gap will disappear. I recommend buying a policy with a deductible that matches your HSA, then increase the deductible—and lower your premiums—as your savings build."

A pilot program introduced HSA-eligible policies to the individual insurance market first, and by 2005 many insurers had such policies ready for the group business market as well. The two HSA-eligible plans work much the same, but group HSA plans may be cheaper and, unlike with individual plans, you usually cannot be denied coverage because of preexisting conditions; your employer may pay none, some, or all of your premiums and may or may not fully or partially fund your linked savings account. Whether you or your employer funds the account, the money remains free from federal and most state taxes.

Another plus is that many of these plans pay 100 percent of medical bills after the deductible has been met, with no copays or coinsurance. According to eHealthInsurance, 85.4 percent of the HSA plans it sold in 2004 paid 100 percent of the bills for office visits, surgery, hospitalization, and lab/X-ray services after the deductible had been met. Some HSA plans also pay certain preventive care expenses, regardless of the deductible.

By the beginning of 2006, HSAs were legally available in forty-four states but were offered in only forty; HSAs will eventually be available in all states. One holdup is that some state laws and regulations must be tweaked or repealed to allow HSA-eligible policies. Another holdup is that insurance companies have simply not designed HSA policies for a few of the states. "The pressure on the market to provide these plans is building," Hurley noted. "It's going to take more time in those states where the regulations and laws need to be changed, but consumers are going to demand it."

The reason for the ballooning demand: a lower price. For a young, single person, an HSA-eligible policy can cost as little as $100 a month or less, sometimes considerably less, compared with up to twice that amount or more for a traditional plan. In a dramatic reversal from the usual trend in health care, HSA premiums fell 17 percent in 2005, compared with the previous year, according to eHealthInsurance. According to the U.S. Department of the Treasury, more than 3 million people have signed up for HSAs or similar plans since they became available.

DON'T CONFUSE HSAs WITH FSAs

Flexible spending accounts, or FSAs, are accounts established through your employer, usually up to a maximum of $5,000, that are not taxed and allow you to pay for out-of-pocket medical expenses with tax-free dollars, which can save you money depending on your tax bracket. Some workers are hesitant to open FSAs because, unlike HSAs, money you don't spend in a given year cannot be carried over to the next year; the Internal Revenue Service takes it. For 2005, the U.S. Treasury allowed companies to extend the spending deadline until March 16, 2006, but only about half the nation's largest companies agreed to the grace period. Generally, you cannot have both an HSA and an FSA, but there can be complex exceptions. Check with your company's human resources department.

FSAs can be used for a lot of medical expenses not covered by insurance, including the copay on prescription drugs and items like prescription sunglasses. If you know you are going to have out-of-pocket expenses, say a lot of dental work that may not be fully covered by your insurance, an FSA makes sense. If you plan carefully, you should exhaust your FSA by year's end. If you don't, you either forgo the money or scramble at the last minute to spend it. One result is that a lot of designer sunglasses get purchased in late December! While FSAs can benefit individuals with out-of-pocket medical expenses, it is this use-it-or-lose-it feature that makes them dubious public policy. Forcing people to buy things like designer eyewear or else forfeit their money is not exactly a prudent use of health-care dollars.

PROS AND CONS OF HSAs

Many political conservatives like HSAs as free-market alternatives to government-supported insurance; President George W. Bush often cites them as one of his major health-care achievements.

HSA critics argue that the tax benefits of the plans favor higher-income people who can afford to fund the accounts and those with good health, usually younger people, whose accounts can build and exceed the deductibles. Sick patients, in contrast, would quickly use up their deductible and have little incentive to save on medical costs. There is also concern that the high deductibles may lead people to neglect routine preventive care if they have to spend their own money on it. As Dr. Barbara Starfield mentioned in chapter 1, such up-front expenses cut down equally on necessary and unnecessary care. In addition, there is no help for those who can't afford even less-expensive premiums.

Critics also contend that as young and healthy workers switch to HSAs, the cost of traditional plans for older workers will increase because of the problem of adverse selection; in other words, there will be fewer younger people in non-HSA plans to subsidize the care of older, less-healthy employees. HSAs represent a break from the traditional idea of shared risk that has long been the hallmark of health insurance in the United States. Instead, consumer-directed health care gives a possible financial reward to the healthy in exchange for an extra, and potentially onerous, burden on the sick.

The plans, of course, do nothing for people who can't get individual insurance because of preexisting conditions. Robert Hurley of eHealthInsurance estimates that 15 to 18 percent of the population fall into this category. "The problem of those who truly can't afford any insurance is a whole other issue," he notes. While Hurley acknowledges that the government may have to step in to help some of these individuals who can't get coverage in the private market, he is optimistic that HSAs will put insurance within the reach of more people. "If you look at the total number of uninsured, around half could actually afford health insurance but don't buy it," he said. "Why? I believe the reason is that they think the premiums are so high they are just flushing money down a black hole." Hurley thinks that lower HSA premiums are already luring some of the uninsured into the insurance market. For instance, an eHealthInsurance study of the HSAs it sold in 2004, the first year they were available, showed that:

- More than two-thirds of HSA-eligible plan purchasers who were previously uninsured for more than six months had incomes of $50,000 or less.
- A total of 40 percent of HSA-eligible plans were purchased by people with incomes of $50,000 or less.
- Almost 90 percent of HSA-eligible plan purchasers paid $200 or less a month per person.

Hurley also cited two health-care industry studies that indicated that people tend to become more attentive to preventive care if they believe paying for it will save them money in the long run.

Another advantage of an HSA is that you can use the money to pay for health-related expenses that insurance may not cover. These can include weight-loss and smoking-cessation programs, as well as premiums for long-term-care insurance.

"What we're seeing is that these HSAs are bringing the individual consumer back into the health-insurance equation," Hurley said. "One of the biggest challenges for business is the lack of predictability in health-care costs. It's possible we can create a system with

HSAs in which employers will have a more predictable contribution to employee health care."

"WITH AN HSA . . . I'M IN CONTROL"

In 2003, Rich Phillips, an Austin, Texas–based entrepreneur, quit his executive job with a high-technology company to start his own management-consulting firm. Phillips had to face the problem of obtaining health insurance coverage for himself. Because of the availability of the new tax-free health savings accounts linked to high-deductible, low-cost policies, however, his problem was less daunting—and less expensive—than it might have been.

In 2004, Phillips, who was thirty-four, purchased an individual HSA-eligible policy for himself and his family—he and his wife have three children—through eHealthInsurance. The plan cost $380.97 a month and had an annual family deductible of $3,350; a traditional policy would have run between $900 and $1,100 monthly. His HSA policy has no coinsurance; it pays 100 percent of medical bills after the deductible has been met.

One of Phillips's sons recently broke his arm. The bill for medical treatment was $700. Because Phillips had more than that amount remaining on his annual deductible, he had to pay the entire bill himself. "I simply wrote a check for $700 out of my HSA account," he said. "With an HSA, I feel like I'm in control. It shifts the burden to me to make sure I'm not overcharged." He believes doctors and health providers are becoming more aware of HSA policies, and he has been able to get insurance-negotiated discounts for some of the medical bills he has had to pay himself out of his health savings account.

Phillips puts about $280 a month into his HSA, which in a year adds up to his policy's annual deductible of $3,350. After a few years, his account will probably grow to contain more than his annual deductible, and that money will also gain interest.

Phillips believes the HSA is "the future of health care": "It puts more responsibility on consumers but also gives them peace of mind that catastrophic expenses will be covered. The cost for employers is lower, so they can offer the benefit without sacrificing growth. It seems to me a better alternative than socialization and other things that are being put out there as options." Phillips acknowledges that HSAs might not seem attractive to everyone. "The scary thing for a lot of people with these policies is the high deductible," he said. "But I see it as a great way to make me vigilant about my health costs."

A NEW OPTION FOR EMPLOYERS

Rich Phillips's company is among the 42 percent of small businesses with fewer than fifty workers that offer no health coverage to their employees, but as his eight-person company grows, Phillips plans to offer group HSA coverage to his employees and their families. "I can't afford to pay one thousand dollars a month per employee for family coverage," Phillips said. "But I can afford the three or four hundred dollars that these HSA plans cost. And it's very attractive to employees for me to pay one hundred percent of the premiums for them and their families. That's rare these days."

For small businesses, the big attraction of HSA policies is not just their price but also their potential to stabilize a company's outlay for health care. Deena Katz, an independent financial adviser and the president of Evensky & Katz in Coral Gables, Florida, is going to switch to an HSA-eligible group plan for her eighteen employees. Her company's insurance premiums have increased by 35 percent each year for three consecutive years—too much for her bottom line.

Katz's company covers insurance for employees only, not their families, and the company's premiums for traditional coverage are more than $500 a month for each employee. Rather than continue paying for coverage, the company will give each employee $300 a month, which Katz estimates will be more than enough to pay the premium for an individual HSA-eligible policy and leave some money that can be contributed to the linked savings account. The $300 allowance will serve as the company's self-imposed cap on health spending.

The switch will save Evensky & Katz $43,200 a year. "That's a huge amount for a small business," Katz said. "We're not AT&T, so any dollars we can save are important. We're also committed to our staff and want to be able to give them insurance. But it's getting harder. So if I can cap that expense and give employees more flexibility, it's good."

Katz predicts other companies stretched by insurance costs will move rapidly to adopt HSAs. "Health insurance is very expensive for employers," she said. "We're all feeling the crunch. One of the ways the government has tried to attack this problem is to put HSAs in place. They've tried HMOs, which haven't worked very well. No matter how you cut it, costs are going to shift from employer to employee. Health insurance is the biggie, and the older you get the more important it is."

Indeed, Andy Slavitt, the chief executive for consumer solutions at United Healthcare, said his company was seeing increased interest in HSA-eligible plans, particularly from larger companies that are offering the plans as part of a menu of benefits. A 2004 survey by Mercer Human Resource Consulting found that 73 percent of employers said they were at least somewhat likely to offer HSAs, and the giant retailer Wal-Mart started offering HSAs to its workers in October 2005.

But switching solely to HSA plans could be difficult for companies with union contracts or other long-term commitments. Robert Fahlman, the chief operating officer of eHealthInsurance, says the big question is how fast the adoption rate among small companies for HSA-eligible policies will be in the next three to five years. "My gut tells me it will take off in a significant way," Fahlman said, "because its win-win for both employers and employees. Once the market understands how these plans work, it's going to migrate to them."

HSAs FOR YOUNG ADULTS

As we saw in chapter 1, young adults are a big block of the uninsured population. Half of those between ages eighteen and twenty-four have no coverage. According to the Commonwealth Fund, the number of people between the ages of nineteen and twenty-nine with no health insurance jumped by 2.2 million between 2000 and 2003. In addition, 38 percent of young adults who graduated from college between 1996 and 2000—and thus were no longer covered under their parents' policies—had a period of time when they were uninsured in the year following graduation. When people are young and healthy, it is inviting to think of insurance as a luxury, not a necessity. Such a youthful "sense of invincibility," however, is also an invitation to financial disaster. Just ask the uninsured college student who found herself thousands of dollars in debt after a blister on her heel led to blood poisoning and other complications requiring hospitalization. Or another student who decided to go without his student insurance while he took time off from school to work. He broke his foot and, stuck with hundreds of dollars in medical bills, was unable to get all the physical therapy he needed. The "invincibility" issue, though, may be a bit overblown; various data indicate that people under age thirty, when offered coverage, accept it at pretty much the same rate as older age groups. It's most likely that younger adults are uninsured for the same reason as older ones: Their employers do not provide insurance, and they feel they cannot afford it on their own.

In the states where they are available, individual HSA-eligible policies could be key in closing this coverage gap for many young adults. Because of their higher deductibles, the policies are considerably less expensive than traditional ones. In addition, younger people with fewer or no preexisting conditions face a much easier time qualifying for individual health insurance than older folks. In fact, as businesses have raised the employee costs for insurance, some young and healthy workers have declined their company's group coverage and actually saved money by buying individual HSAs.

At the eHealthInsurance Web site (www.ehealthinsurance.com), visitors can get quotes for premiums anonymously and compare plans in every state. All you have to provide is your zip code, birth date, gender, number of dependents, whether you are a smoker, and whether you are a student. There are other online brokers that provide such quotes, but some—like www.insure.com—require you to give your name and fill out a health questionnaire in order to get a quote.

I checked the eHealthInsurance site for some HSA plans, using my home zip code in Manhattan, Kansas. For a twenty-two-year-old male, a total of nine HSA-eligible policies were offered, ranging in price from $66.17 a month to $125.17 a month; a traditional plan (with a $500 deductible, $25 copayment for doctor's visits, and 20 percent coinsurance) could run more than $175 a month. (For a fifty-year-old male with no preexisting condition issues, the same HSA policies would run from $154.86 to $314.63 a month; a comparable traditional policy could run as much as $388.73 a month.)

The least expensive HSA-eligible policy had a $5,000 annual deductible. Since the maximum an individual can contribute tax free to an HSA each year is $2,700, this would mean if the twenty-two-year-old had an expensive illness during the first year the policy was in effect, he would have to pay the difference, $2,300—and it would not be from his tax-free funds, which might not have accrued in the account yet. However, after two or three healthy years in a row—not unusual for a twenty-two-year-old—he would have more than enough in the HSA to cover the $5,000 deductible. In addition, this particular policy, like the Phillips family's policy, had no coinsurance requirement, which means it would pay 100 percent of bills after the deductible was met.

Other policies had lower deductibles, ranging from $1,500 to $2,600. Some required a 20 percent coinsurance payment after the deductible had been met, up to the policy's maximum out-of-pocket amount, typically $2,000 for an individual and $4,000 for a family. Most of the HSA plans were PPOs, or preferred provider organizations, covered prescription drugs, and had a lifetime benefit cap of $5 million.

There were traditional plans that were less expensive than even the cheapest HSA-eligible plan. However, the plans had the same $5,000 deductible without the benefit of a tax-free account to pay it, as well as 20 percent coinsurance and $30 copays for doctor's visits. Some of these policies also had higher out-of-pocket limits.

As is clear from the preceding examples, as well as examples in the next chapter that look at policies and prices in a number of states across the country, HSAs, even with their high deductibles, can save you money on premiums—sometimes a lot of money. Another plus is that many of these plans pay 100 percent of medical bills after the deductible has been met, with no copays or coinsurance. Remember, according to eHealthInsurance, 85.4 percent of the plans it sold in 2004 paid 100 percent of the bills for office visits, surgery, hospitalization, and lab/X-ray services after the deductible had been met. Some HSA plans also pay certain preventive-care expenses, regardless of the deductible.

AN HSA PLAN FOR A FAMILY OF FOUR

Let's now consider the example, provided by eHealthInsurance, of a couple in their midthirties, with two grade-school-age children, living in Chicago, Illinois. A typical fee-for-service (indemnity) health insurance plan—the most expensive kind—for them would cost $9,984 a year, or $832 a month.

Now assume the family bought an HSA-eligible plan with an annual premium of only $2,966, or $247 a month, with a deductible of

$5,000. That means they can make a tax-free contribution to the HSA for up to the amount of the deductible. Using a federal tax rate of 25 percent and a state tax rate of 3 percent, the family will save $1,400 on taxes. If the HSA plan's annual premium and the HSA contribution are subtracted from the $9,984 that the traditional plan costs, that would provide additional savings of $2,018 a year. The premium difference alone between the two plans—$7,018—is more than enough to fund the HSA plan's linked savings account.

For any medical bills, however, they will first have to spend $5,000 in a given year out of their HSA; only then will their insurance kick in. Depending on their policy, they could still face some copayment or coinsurance costs. However, by law, their maximum out-of-pocket annual expenses are $10,500. If they have no big expense for two or three years, their HSA—growing at the rate of $5,000 a year, plus investment earnings—would easily cover that maximum. Of course, like most people who buy HSA-eligible policies, they could select a plan that pays 100 percent of medical bills after they meet the deductible. They can keep the part of the HSA they don't spend on health care, but they can't spend it on anything else without paying taxes plus a 10 percent penalty. Remember, too, that at age sixty-five, when they become eligible for Medicare, the couple can withdraw the money without penalty and spend it on anything they want, although they must pay taxes on it. (If they use the money for medical expenses, it is not taxed.)

How much money are we talking about? It depends on how much the couple spends each year on medical care. The eHealthInsurance case study assumes they fully fund their HSA each year and spend only $2,000 of their $5,000 HSA each year on medical care. This leaves $3,000 in the account to build year to year. After thirty years, with an assumed 4 percent return, their HSA total would grow to $174,091. Is $2,000 a year a reasonable amount to expect a family of four to spend for health care? Maybe, at least in the younger years. According to recent government figures, the average medical expenses for people under age sixty-five are $2,138 a year. That amount, however, is an average and is clearly lower for younger people and higher for older people. Approximately 73 percent of Americans incur less than $500 a year in medical expenses. Even if the couple in eHealth-Insurance's example has to use all the money they contribute one year, they will still have spent less on health care than with the traditional policy if their HSA pays 100 percent after the deductible is met. In addition, they have had increased control over how their health-care dollars are spent.

IS AN HSA FOR YOU?

Critics of HSAs have described them as bad public policy because they do little for the root problems of the health-care crisis engulfing America. For certain people, however, they can be very advantageous. You should seriously consider an HSA-eligible policy—whether offered by your employer or purchased privately—if you are relatively healthy and are seeking a tax shelter for some of your income. HSAs are also useful if you are looking for a lower-cost way to protect yourself from the financial consequences of a catastrophic illness and are less concerned about relatively minor medical expenses such as visits to a doctor's office. And if your employer pays the premium *and* funds the health savings account linked to the plan—employers are allowed to do both, but most don't—you should take advantage of it.

However, you should be wary of HSA policies if you or someone in your family has a chronic health condition. First off, you probably will only be able to get a group HSA plan offered through your job so that the preexisting conditions are covered. Also, you will likely be forced to use all of your deductible every year to cover your bills. You may fare better financially and have fewer headaches with a traditional policy, depending on the HSA's deductible, copayments, and coinsurance.

Let's work through a couple of comparisons. In all cases, the assumption is that a policy's out-of-pocket maximum includes the deductible. (This is true with HSAs but not with all traditional policies.)

Take the case of a thirty-five-year-old healthy male living in Phoenixville, Pennsylvania, a suburb of Philadelphia. Let's say his company offers him an HSA with a $2,000 deductible and a coinsurance payment of 20 percent up to an out-of-pocket maximum of $4,000. The company pays the monthly premiums, but the worker must use his own money to fund the policy's $2,000 tax-free account. Assuming his taxes total approximately 30 percent, he will save $600 in taxes each year on the $2,000 he puts into the account. Let's further assume his medical bills for an annual physical and minor ailments like colds or the flu run $500 a year. That means that at the end of the year he has $1,500 left in his account, he has spent $500, and he has saved $600 in taxes. He is ahead by $100, plus he has the $1,500 balance in his account that will carry over year to year. (In a traditional plan with, say, a $500 deductible, he would simply be out $500.) The next year he will be able to add another $2,000 to his tax-free account and save another $600 in taxes. Such a plan clearly benefits him. In a few years he could have more than enough in his account to pay the full deductible and full coinsurance—the two would total $4,000 a year—if he developed a costly health problem. Of course, if he developed a long-term chronic condition that forced him to spend the entire out-of-pocket maximum every year for several years, he could quickly wipe out his gains. In such a case, he would be much better off with an HSA policy that paid 100 percent after his deductible had been met, assuming his employer offered one, because he would be spending $2,000 a year instead of $4,000. Remember, though, he is saving $600 a year in taxes, so the $4,000 is actually only $3,400.

Now suppose our employee has a chronic health condition and knows from the beginning that each year he will spend the out-of-pocket maximum. Conventional coverage might be better for him.

The assumed $500 deductible is lower, and traditional group plans may have a lower out-of-pocket maximum, perhaps $2,000 or less. This would leave him responsible for $2,500 a year or less; if you add the $600 he will *not* be saving in taxes, the total is $3,100 or less. With a traditional policy, he would have to spend only $500 before insurance kicks in; with the HSA, he would have to spend $2,000 first. In addition, traditional plans usually include prescription drug benefits that start right away, regardless of the deductible or coinsurance, which could make a big difference for someone with chronic problems. On the other hand, there are usually copayments for doctor visits in traditional plans that can run from $5 to $30 or more and may not count toward the out-of-pocket maximum. Keep in mind, too, that if you're paying the premium instead of your employer—like the couple in eHealthInsurance's case study—you could still come out ahead with an HSA even if you are chronically ill.

As you can see from these hypothetical examples, you're simply going to have to sit down with a calculator and compare different outcomes from whatever health plans you are offered or are able to buy on your own. EHealthInsurance's Web site can help, as can www.hsainsider.com, a site that provides insurance industry information on HSAs. Perhaps you fall somewhere in the middle in terms of health problems. Certainly, if you have a chronic health issue that will always force you to use 100 percent of your HSA tax-free savings each year, you should be wary. The *Wall Street Journal* cited the problem of those with HSAs who have just enough health expenses that they reach their deductible by the end of each year and have to start over again in January; they never pay the maximum out-of-pocket and never benefit from coverage that kicks in after that. A June 2005 study by McKinsey & Company indicated that 56 percent of patients with consumer-directed health plans were less satisfied with them than with their previous health plans; in one company surveyed, that dissatisfaction ran as high as 76 percent. (In fairness, however, it should be pointed out that most participants in the study were not covered under HSAs but under earlier, similar plans called health reimbursement accounts that were somewhat less tax-advantageous.) Another survey, released jointly by the Employee Benefit Research Institute and the Commonwealth Fund in December 2005, found that 63 percent of those surveyed were extremely or very satisfied with their traditional comprehensive health insurance, compared with 33 percent among those with high-deductible health plans like HSAs. The same survey also found that about a third of the people making less than $50,000 a year who were enrolled in these plans reported delaying or avoiding health care because of costs, compared with 17 percent in traditional plans. Karen Davis, president of the Commonwealth Fund, issued the following comment with the survey: "These findings provide evidence that high-deductible and consumer-driven plans may undermine the two basic purposes of health insurance: to reduce financial barriers to needed care and protect against high out-of-pocket cost burdens for patients. Enrollees with low incomes or with health problems are particularly vulnerable to spending a high proportion of income on medical expenses under these types of plans."

Before you sign up for an HSA, you should keep the following points in mind:

Make sure you have sufficient income to fund your HSA account and fully understand what your costs will be. A tax-free savings benefit doesn't mean much if you can't afford to save the money. If you can't fund the account, you certainly aren't going to be able to afford the hundreds or thousands of dollars you will have to pay up front if you get sick. Remember, one of the main concepts driving HSAs is the shifting of costs to you from your employer or insurer.

Make an assessment of your annual health expenses and the state of your health. Is there a history of a particular illness in your family to which you might be unusually susceptible later in life that over several years could wipe out your HSA? Are you the kind of person who might skimp on health care if you have to spend your own money for it? Skipping a visit to the doctor if you have a sinus headache might make sense; waiting to see if a changed skin lesion worsens, or if chest pains are simple indigestion, may not.

Look for a policy that pays 100 percent of your medical expenses after the deductible has been met. Otherwise, you could face thousands of dollars in charges for copayments and coinsurance. If you're buying coverage on your own, the difference in premiums is not that great. In the example of the twenty-two-year-old male in Kansas, HSA policies that pay 100 percent after the deductible can be as little as $15 a month more than those that don't. If you do—or must—select a policy with copays and coinsurance, try to keep the out-of-pocket maximum as low as possible. Remember, though, that federal law governing HSAs limits the maximum out-of-pocket expense for an individual to $5,250 and for a family, $10,500.

Check that a policy has a lifetime maximum of at least $1 million; $3 million to $5 million would be better.

Be aware that most HSA policies are linked to PPOs, or preferred provider organizations. This means that if you choose to go to a doctor or hospital outside the network, you must pay more even if you have met your deductible. (A policy that pays 80 percent after the deductible is met might pay only 60 percent for out-of-network services.) Make sure your doctors are part of the policy's PPO.

Explain to your doctor that you have an HSA and will probably be paying most of his or her bills yourself. Ask for a discount similar to that given to patients whose bills are paid directly by an insurance company. Because these policies are relatively new, however, many doctors don't yet understand them. Also, individuals don't have the bargaining clout of big insurers, and doctors' contracts with insurers may put limits on the discounts they can give to people who are paying their own way. If you're shy or nervous about discussing prices with your doctor, you might be better off with a traditional plan. After all, one of the ideas behind HSAs is that they will force you to seek out the best prices.

Be aware that HSAs often don't provide prescription drug coverage until you have met your deductible. Even after you have met the deductible, you may not have a traditional prescription card that requires a copayment. You may have to pay for the drugs up front and submit the bills to your insurance carrier.

Check whether your HSA will pay for preventative care, regardless of the deductible.

Brace yourself for bookkeeping and paperwork hassles. You'll need to keep copies of bills and payments, as well as file claim forms. Lack of organization and attention to details can cost you money. (Chapter 7 provides some pointers on managing insurance claims and other paperwork.)

Understand that the money you put into your health savings account can be at risk, especially if it's invested in stocks. True, stocks carry the potential of greater returns, but they also carry the risk of losing money. Watch out for fees charged for the accounts by banks and financial services companies. These can run as much as $45 or more during the first year of a new account. Banks love HSAs—for good reasons. By 2010, HSAs will generate $800 million in management fees and $1.2 billion in transaction fees each year, according to DiamondCluster International, a management consulting firm in Chicago.

SOUTH AFRICA'S EXPERIENCE WITH HSAs

In chapter 1, I noted that some health-care experts predict that HSAs, because they do not solve the underlying problems causing our health-care crisis and are too dependent on market forces, will eventually fail to contain costs, repeating the history of HMOs in the 1980s and 1990s. When HSAs meet their price-control ceiling, true health-care reform—which deals with the problems of the uninsured and the underinsured—might finally be possible.

One country that has already gone where we are headed is South Africa, the only other industrialized nation besides the United States that does not guarantee health care to its citizens. The South African insurance market was deregulated in 1994, giving rise to many companies offering consumer-directed health-care plans similar to HSAs. One result, according to David Adler's November 2005 article in the *New Republic*, is that these insurers have cherry-picked healthy people for such plans, which "work best if you have little need to go to the doctor." Sicker people have had to rely on traditional plans.

Adler contends that South Africa's experience with consumer-directed health plans may be ending. In 2002, the nation's Department of Health conducted an inquiry into its health system, concluding that HSAs should be phased out. Adler quotes from the study: *"The focus of health policy needs to be on risk-sharing and cost containment. None of these key health policy objectives can be achieved through medical savings accounts"* (italics in original).

Adler concludes: "South Africa is now in the process of reregulating the health care industry and moving away from medical savings accounts. South Africa gives us a chance to look before we leap—and hopefully step back from the edge."

If health care were left to market forces, certain segments of our society simply would never have coverage. Medicare was created because the private insurance industry walked away from the market for older people, just as today it is walking away from the market for people with preexisting conditions. And what about those who can't afford insurance premiums in this new world of consumer-directed health care? Dr. Arnold Relman, the Harvard Medical School professor emeritus and former editor of the *New England Journal of Medicine,* wrote in the *New Republic*: "'Consumer-driven' plans are unrealistic and unfair, and they are not likely to be politically viable in the long run. There is some understandable support for the idea that individuals should be more responsible for the cost of elective or optional medical services, but most people believe that the availability of needed services should not depend on ability to pay. We are a wealthy society, and decency requires that we make equitable arrangements to ensure at least minimally adequate health care for all—a goal that is beyond the scope of market forces."

5

The State of Your Health and the State Where You Live

Trying to buy an individual policy is tough; thirty to forty percent of the people we try to place are getting turned down.

—STEPHEN L. WYSS, MANAGING DIRECTOR OF
AFFINITY GROUP UNDERWRITERS

Until recently, most people have been provided with health insurance through their jobs and have given little thought to the cost. But that era is rapidly coming to an end. Companies, faced with the hit of rising health expenses on their budgets, are shifting costs onto employees, cutting back on coverage, or both, usually through increased premium-sharing by workers, increased copayments for prescription drugs and medical services, and higher annual deductibles. Companies have also started moving to policies linked to health savings accounts (discussed in chapter 4). All these changes and increases have taken a bite out of employees' disposable incomes. While companies often offer the cheapest access to health insurance, they are not required by law to provide coverage to employees; many smaller businesses, based on the costs alone, do not. We have created a system in which most people can get affordable insurance only through their jobs, yet employers are not required to provide coverage—and many can no longer afford to.

Consider what happens to workers who have employer-provided insurance and become too sick to work or are injured and can't work. They most commonly lose their insurance—just when they need it the most. While many people can continue their coverage under COBRA, the extra, and often heavy, financial burden on someone who has just lost his or her source of income is tough. You can easily find yourself hit with a triple whammy: sick or injured, unable to work, and suddenly without health coverage or burdened with a big insurance premium. Indeed, a breakdown of data on the uninsured demonstrates that 80 percent of the nation's approximately 32 million adults without insurance work, but their companies do not offer health insurance to employees or their job does not qualify for the employer's coverage.

THE INSURANCE LAWS IN YOUR STATE

The biggest health insurance challenge involves people who have no coverage through their jobs and are forced to purchase individual insurance, which can carry high prices and harsh limitations on preexisting conditions. Insurance companies in all but a few states can exclude health problems related to preexisting conditions from coverage or refuse to cover a person at all. A preexisting condition can make it extremely difficult—often impossible—to get coverage under an individual policy.

Your access to an individual policy depends in large part on the state of your finances, the state of your health, and the state where you live. The states have varying laws that govern access to individual health insurance. The first step in shopping for an individual policy is finding out if you live in a state with a *guaranteed-issue law* or *community rating*. Guaranteed-issue laws require that any insurance companies offering individual policies to residents in a state have to sell insurance to all regardless of preexisting conditions. As of 2006, five states carry these laws: Maine, Massachusetts, New Jersey, New York, and Vermont. (In April 2006, Massachusetts passed a law guaranteeing near-universal coverage, but it doesn't fully take effect until 2007.) There is an obvious problem, however, with guaranteed-issue laws: People can wait until they are sick to buy insurance. "It's like buying homeowner's insurance when your house is on fire," said Robert Hurley of eHealthInsurance. Because insurers in these states have to take all comers, regardless of health conditions, the policies are comparatively expensive for everyone, and there can be a waiting period before coverage becomes active for those who do not have prior insurance. These higher premiums put insurance out of financial reach for more people. Unfortunately, guaranteed issue doesn't mean guaranteed affordability.

If you are healthy and have no preexisting medical conditions, buying individual insurance should not be difficult in a state without guaranteed-issue laws. It will certainly be less expensive. Insurance underwriters, however, are very risk-adverse whenever they are allowed to be, so they will look for any opening to exclude a preexisting condition—and perhaps deny coverage altogether. "Trying to buy an individual policy is tough; thirty to forty percent of the people we try to place are getting turned down," said Stephen L. Wyss, the managing director of Affinity Group Underwriters. If an insurer agrees to cover you but excludes a preexisting condition from the coverage, shop around. For example, a policy that doesn't cover a stroke or heart disease because you have high blood pressure may not be worth the premiums.

The good news is that though state laws governing insurance vary widely, once you are issued a policy it can't be canceled unless your insurer stops doing business in your state. (There are rare exceptions, all worth appealing.) Also, you generally cannot be singled out for a rate increase if you develop a health problem; rates must be increased for your entire class, which usually refers to your age, but can include other groupings such as geography. A very helpful Web site run by the Georgetown University Health Policy Institute (www.healthinsuranceinfo.net) can provide you with current information on insurance rules in various states. Another site with state-by-state rules and consumer information is www.naic.org, which is operated by the National Association of Insurance Commissioners.

The other major consideration in buying an individual policy is community rating. Most states allow insurers to base the initial premiums charged for individual policies on a client's health and age. The five "guaranteed-issue" states—Maine, Massachusetts, New Jersey, New York, and Vermont—require that insurers charge all "community residents" the same premium, regardless of their health status. New York and New Jersey have virtually no exceptions that would allow for premium differences, while in Maine, Massachusetts, and Vermont, there can be limited premium differences depending on your age, occupation, and smoking status. Premiums in the five guaranteed-issue states are uniform and high, so there are only modest differences among plans offered by rival insurance companies, and many health insurers refuse to sell policies in the five states, which exacerbates the lack of competition.

But if you suffer from preexisting conditions that are closing you out of coverage elsewhere, it may pay to move to a guaranteed-issue state rather than face potentially bankrupting medical costs from an excluded condition down the road. That doesn't have to be a big move if you live near the border of a guaranteed-issue state; you could relocate and perhaps even keep your job in your former state. By the same token, if you are healthy and live and work in a guaranteed-issue state like New York and New Jersey, where individual premiums are high, you could move to a nearby state with less expensive premiums and commute to your job. Premiums in Pennsylvania and Delaware, for example, are much less than in New Jersey; Connecticut is less than New York. Of course, you would have the extra expense and hassle of a longer commute, but the savings could be worth it. You would also have to consider any general cost-of-living differences.

SHOPPING FOR INSURANCE

It may seem as though insurance providers make their plans complex specifically so you can't compare them side by side as you would, say, a life insurance policy. To help get a handle on the differences in coverage among various kinds of individual health insurance policies, I asked eHealthInsurance, the big online insurance broker, to provide some quotes for three kinds of policies in a sampling of U.S. cities. The quotes are for the least expensive monthly premiums in five different states for HMO, PPO, and HSA-eligible policies. Because fee-for-service policies are much more expensive than other options, I have not included quotes for these plans. One of the states included in the comparisons is New Jersey, a guaranteed-issue and community-rating state; in early 2006, individual HSA policies were not yet being offered there, although employer-sponsored group HSA polices were already available. The examples give a snapshot of the cheapest policies available, regardless of the deductible, which can be as high as $10,000. A different comparison, by deductible or benefits, for instance, would yield a very different ranking, and comparing low-premium policies with low-deductible policies can lead to very confusing results. Once you get a feel for how to compare policies by a premium-price standard, you can decide which element of a policy is most important to you and shop accordingly. Keep in mind that the prices in this and other chapters will likely have changed by the time this book is published; it is the relative differences among them that will help you untangle the costs for your own coverage.

Because quotes vary widely based on age, gender, and family situation, I have included comparisons for eight different scenarios so that you will also gain a sense for the general price ranges you will encounter at different stages of life. For each person or family, the lowest monthly premiums for an HMO, a PPO, and an HSA-eligible plan are listed. At the time these quotes were run, eHealthInsurance did not offer HMO plans in Chicago, so the HMO price there reflects a PPO plan with a low deductible and no copayments.

Twenty-five-Year-Old Single Male

	HMO	PPO	HSA
Springfield, NJ	$410.91	$374.67	NA
San Jose, CA	88.00	36.00	$36.00
Chicago, IL	210.35	43.20	60.00
Phoenix, AZ	70.00	38.12	41.69
Atlanta, GA	53.00	42.43	53.00

Twenty-five-Year-Old Single Female

	HMO	PPO	HSA
Springfield, NJ	$410.91	$374.67	NA
San Jose, CA	88.00	36.00	$36.00
Chicago, IL	275.05	45.90	62.00
Phoenix, AZ	192.00	49.44	51.90
Atlanta, GA	78.00	59.40	78.00

Two Twenty-five-Year-Old Adults with Two Children, Ages Three and Six

	HMO	PPO	HSA
Springfield, NJ	$1,244.46	$1,067.81	NA
San Jose, CA	258.00	113.00	$113.00
Chicago, IL	843.41	140.00	140.00
Phoenix, AZ	398.00	133.40	108.90
Atlanta, GA	227.00	165.10	211.09

Two Thirty-five-Year-Old Adults with Two Children, Ages Five and Eight

	HMO	PPO	HSA
Springfield, NJ	$1,244.46	$1,067.81	NA
San Jose, CA	333.00	146.00	$207.00
Chicago, IL	984.21	165.00	165.00
Phoenix, AZ	434.00	161.80	132.78
Atlanta, GA	282.00	180.66	245.03

Single Forty-Year-Old Male

	HMO	PPO	HSA
Springfield, NJ	$410.91	$374.67	NA
San Jose, CA	191.00	77.00	$86.00
Chicago, IL	347.85	78.49	93.00
Phoenix, AZ	143.00	61.84	66.36
Atlanta, GA	75.00	62.22	75.00

Single Forty-Year-Old Female

	HMO	PPO	HSA
Springfield, NJ	$410.91	$374.67	NA
San Jose, CA	191.00	77.00	$86.00
Chicago, IL	403.51	75.60	118.00
Phoenix, AZ	197.00	78.39	82.52
Atlanta, GA	122.00	96.59	121.00

Married Couple, Each Forty-eight Years Old

	HMO	PPO	HSA
Springfield, NJ	$878.79	$749.34	NA
San Jose, CA	371.00	171.00	$237.00
Chicago, IL	918.02	144.00	144.00
Phoenix, AZ	417.00	182.25	148.03
Atlanta, GA	249.00	215.48	174.06

Married Couple, Each Fifty-five Years Old

	HMO	PPO	HSA
Springfield, NJ	$878.79	$749.34	NA
San Jose, CA	585.00	329.00	$403.00
Chicago, IL	963.69	264.00	221.00
Phoenix, AZ	599.00	355.25	173.57
Atlanta, GA	444.00	296.58	230.82

If a quick look at these prices leaves you puzzled, don't worry; even health insurance brokers can have trouble sorting them out. Add in comparisons based on benefit details, which are available on eHealthInsurance's Web site, and they get even more confusing. In many cases, HSAs are more expensive than PPOs because the PPOs have higher deductibles; the PPOs do not, of course, come with a tax-free savings account, which effectively lowers the HSA premium come tax time—depending on your income. And in some cases, the least expensive HSA plan is just an HSA-eligible version of the least expensive HMO or PPO.

One of the factors affecting price differences from state to state is the degree to which a state mandates coverage. You can see right away the effects that guaranteed-issue laws have on insurance prices in New Jersey; the prices there are double or more—sometimes much more—than those in other geographic areas. In addition, some states require that certain medical procedures be covered. These mandates may cover basic traditional medical services and provide valuable protections for policyholders; they may also include care from providers like chiropractors and podiatrists as well as services like acupuncture, alcohol abuse treatment, or pastoral counseling. But the more mandates, the higher the insurance premiums. The Council for Affordable Health Insurance, an advocacy group for insurers, estimates that state mandates increase the cost of coverage from 20 to 50 percent. You can find an up-to-date list of state mandates at the council's Web site (www.cahi.org). From the home page, click on "Publications & Resources."

Let's look more closely at the coverage details of the three least expensive insurance policies in San Jose, California, for the married couple, each forty-eight years old. Of an HMO, PPO, and HSA, the HMO is the most expensive at $371 a month; the PPO is the cheapest at $171, and the HSA falls between, at $237. That the HMO is the most expensive makes some sense since it has no coinsurance, although unlike many HMOs, it has a deductible of $1,500 per person ($3,000 for both). The annual cost of the plan will tally up to $4,452 plus the deductible and $30 copays for each office visit after the deductible is met. The PPO has a $1,500 deductible for each individual ($3,000 for both), coinsurance payments of 25 percent, and maximum out-of-pocket expenses of $4,000 per individual ($8,000 for both). So the annual cost will be $2,052 plus 100 percent of medical costs up to $1,500 for each person, possibly adding a whopping $8,000 if both the husband and wife meet their out-of-pocket maximums. The HSA, which is $66 a month more expensive than the PPO, has a family deductible of $5,000, coinsurance payments of 30 percent, and an out-of-pocket maximum of $10,500, the amount set by law. That's $2,844 per year plus up to $10,500 more—with higher deductibles and coinsurance. And HSAs are supposed to be the option for saving money! The HSA pays 70 percent of prescription drugs after the deductible is met; the other two policies do not cover prescriptions. Still, why is the HSA almost 40 percent more expensive than the PPO? Both carry the same lifetime maximum benefit of $6 million. With the HSA, the couple saves the taxes on the money they contributed to the savings account to pay the plan's deductible of $5,000, which could make the HSA somewhat less expensive, depending on their income bracket.

Now multiply this whole exercise by thirty to get a sense of the difficulty inherent in shopping for a policy. EHealthInsurance lists ninety individual insurance plans, including sixteen HSAs, available in California alone. Choice is good, but it can also be overwhelming. Before you start comparing the numbers for yourself, you should create a profile of your expected medical needs over the next five years. (Lots of office visits for growing kids? High-ticket treatments for a preexisting condition? A lot of brand-name drug prescriptions?) Then you will be in a position to match your health needs—copayments for office visits rather than coinsurance; a relatively low deductible, since you will likely hit your out-of-pocket maximum; or prescription coverage—to the benefits offered at the price you can pay.

You may want to consult an insurance broker in your area to help you sort this out. (Although eHealthInsurance is online, the company has a toll-free number [800-977-8860] you can call for personal assistance.) Keep in mind, though, that when brokers sell an insurance policy, the company pays them a commission. These commissions vary, and some brokers may push high-commission policies that are more in their interest than in yours. So in the end, you will still want to check your options online against a policy recommended by a broker.

THE MOST AFFORDABLE CITIES FOR YOUR HEALTH

EHealthInsurance has compiled some illuminating data on the fifty most affordable major cities for buying health insurance. The full reports can be accessed on the company's Web site (www.ehealth insurance.com): click on "About Us" on the home page, then "News," and then "Reports."

The ranking of cities for individual coverage assumes the applicant is thirty years old, a nonsmoker, and has no preexisting conditions. The policies have a maximum deductible of $1,000 and coinsurance of 20 percent, and an average annual out-of-pocket maximum of $3,286. (It's almost impossible to find a perfect apples-to-apples comparison.) The twelve cheapest cities and the average monthly premiums for an individual:

1. Long Beach, California ($54.00)
2. Sacramento, California ($56.00)
   Fresno, California ($56.00)
4. San Diego, California ($57.00)
5. Columbus, Ohio ($57.91)
6. San Jose, California ($58.00)
   San Francisco, California ($58.00)
   Oakland, California ($58.00)
9. Mesa, Arizona ($58.74)
10. Tucson, Arizona ($58.77)
11. Omaha, Nebraska ($60.34)
12. Los Angeles, California ($63.00)

The five most expensive cities for individual coverage:

5. Houston, Texas ($146.28)
4. Dallas, Texas ($146.42)
3. Miami, Florida ($151.20)
2. Boston, Massachusetts ($267.57)
1. New York, New York ($334.00)

The ranking for family coverage assumes the family comprises two parents, ages thirty-seven and thirty-five, and two children, ages nine and eleven. It also assumes neither parent smokes and no one has pre-existing conditions. The policies have a maximum deductible of $2,000, coinsurance of 20 percent, and maximum out-of-pocket expenses ranging from $4,000 to $10,000 a year. The fifteen cheapest cities:

1. Kansas City, Missouri ($171.86)
2. Long Beach, California ($180.00)
3. Columbus, Ohio ($182.28)
4. Tucson, Arizona ($184.88)
   Mesa, Arizona ($184.88)

6. San Jose, California ($190.00)
   San Francisco, California ($190.00)
   Oakland, California ($190.00)
   Sacramento, California ($190.00)
   Fresno, California ($190.00)
11. Omaha, Nebraska ($190.09)
12. San Diego, California ($199.00)
13. Cleveland, Ohio ($208.32)
14. Phoenix, Arizona ($210.92)
15. Los Angeles, California ($212.00)

The five most expensive cities for family coverage:

5. Miami, Florida ($524.18)
4. Minneapolis, Minnesota ($529.00)
3. Charlotte, North Carolina ($541.85)
2. New York, New York ($712.77)
1. Boston, Massachusetts ($767.30)

These rankings clearly demonstrate how competitive the market for health insurance is in California, in part because of the state's relatively light regulations.

MEDICAID IS AN OPTION

All this information about shopping state-by-state is of little use if you can't afford premiums even in the cheapest, most competitive insurance markets or can't qualify for individual coverage because of preexisting conditions.

The affordability barrier to coverage can be insurmountable for lower-income workers, especially those with children, who do not qualify for Medicaid. But if you feel the premiums in your state are too high for your budget, don't assume you don't qualify for

Medicaid. A good source of information about Medicaid eligibility is your state's official Web site, as well as the Web sites of the National Association of Insurance Commissioners (www.naic.org), Families USA (www.familiesusa.org), and the Kaiser Family Foundation (www.kff.org).

Of course, even if you qualify for Medicaid, you can find yourself facing a maze of regulations, limitations, and cutbacks—depending on the state you live in. In addition, reimbursement rates are so low that many doctors refuse to accept Medicaid patients. One Yonkers, New York, physician complained in a letter to the *New York Times* that when she visited a Medicaid patient in the hospital, she was paid only $7.50 by the program. A dentist told the *Charlotte Observer* that Medicaid payment rates were so low that it was cheaper to provide free services to Medicaid patients than to process the claim forms. The result of payment rates like this, though, is that many patients are left with few treatment choices other than hospital clinics, emergency rooms, and so-called Medicaid mills. A study in the *Journal of the American Medical Association* in 2005 reported that a caller to an ambulatory clinic claiming to have private insurance is almost twice as likely as someone with Medicaid to secure a timely appointment. Ninety-eight percent of clinics screen callers for a source of payment; only 28 percent inquire about the severity of a caller's condition.

States, which have extensive control over who is eligible for Medicaid, are in many cases tightening eligibility restrictions and cutting the number of patients as budgets come under increasing pressure. According to the Kaiser Family Foundation, in 2005:

- All fifty states froze or reduced payment rates for at least one group of providers, including hospitals, physicians, and nursing homes.
- Forty-three states implemented new pharmacy cost controls.

- Eight states imposed new or higher beneficiary copayments.
- Eight states imposed eligibility restrictions.
- Seven states restricted or reduced benefits.

The foundation also points out that Medicaid and other public health programs divide low-income populations into three groups: children, parents of dependent children, and nonparent adults. "Each of the low-income groups," Kaiser reports, "is treated very differently from the others—with children receiving most favored treatment, parents receiving less favorable treatment, and nonparent adults virtually excluded from public health coverage." According to Kaiser, in forty of the fifty states, nonparent adults are ineligible for Medicaid—even if they have no income at all—unless they are severely disabled. The ten states that provide *some* coverage for nondisabled adults are Arizona, Delaware, Hawaii, Massachusetts, Minnesota, New Jersey, New York, Oregon, Vermont, and Washington. The Web sites of the Kaiser Family Foundation and Families USA include up-to-date information on specific Medicaid rules and changes in the various states.

While it's true that some states—most notably, Massachusetts—are taking the lead in instituting their own programs outside of Medicaid to help the uninsured, especially children, get coverage, the effort is by definition piecemeal and certainly not a national solution to a national problem. After all, does a state want to become a magnet for sick people because it offers better coverage? This is not to imply, however, that you should not take advantage of what your state has to offer.

SHORT-TERM FIXES

Because Medicaid eligibility is becoming more difficult, two other options you should consider if you are struggling to afford an individual policy to fit your budget and your medical needs: short-term insurance and coverage through an association.

Short-term insurance is just what its name implies: coverage for a defined period, usually less than a year. The insurance is less expensive, the application process for it is simpler, and the coverage is not as difficult to qualify for as traditional long-term insurance. However—and this is a big however—it commonly does not cover preexisting conditions. Most policies also do not cover preventive care, physicals, or immunizations. Short-term insurance is designed primarily to protect against an unforeseen accident or illness and is ideal for people who are between jobs or waiting for other coverage to start. Warning: Do not buy a short-term insurance plan if you are coming off COBRA coverage and expect to switch to HIPAA guaranteed-issue coverage within the sixty-three days in which you are allowed to do so after you leave COBRA. Buying short-term insurance can make you ineligible for the HIPAA coverage.

Another possible route to health insurance is to join a group. Several trade, fraternal, or professional organizations, many with lax membership rules, offer health insurance to their members. Preexisting conditions, however, will likely be excluded. Only a few years ago, many of these organizations offered their members group insurance that covered preexisting conditions, but too many people with health problems were joining such groups specifically to get the medical coverage. This created an adverse selection that forced insurers to drop the coverage. About the only advantage to association coverage now is the price. "But it's not a huge advantage," according to Stephen Wyss of Affinity Group Underwriters, "so the association health insurance business is dying on the vine." Wyss's company has moved from offering comprehensive insurance to group members to selling groups supplemental limited benefit health policies, typically paying $250 a day if you are hospitalized. "But that's not going to cover a hospital bill," he acknowledges.

THE LAST OPTION: INTO THE HIGH-RISK POOL

If you aren't eligible for COBRA or HIPAA coverage, can't qualify for individual insurance because of preexisting conditions, and your income isn't low enough for you to qualify for Medicaid, your only choice may be a high-risk pool—if your state has one. In such cases, states contract with insurers to fund a pool for normally uninsurable people. Unfortunately, the premiums are usually very high, and there can be waiting lists or outright moratoriums on accepting new participants. In some states, the high-risk pool is the HIPAA option for those coming off COBRA coverage, and in those cases, you can't be turned down. Across the board, high-risk pools are painful evidence of the failure of our health-care system and epitomize how adverse selection creates steep tiers of coverage that hurt the people who most need insurance.

According to data from the Kaiser Family Foundation, as of 2006 thirty-four states offered high-risk pools or some equivalent. Guaranteed-issue states don't need high-risk pools, of course. The eleven states that don't ensure coverage for high-risk individuals are Arizona, Delaware, Georgia, Hawaii, Michigan, Nevada, North Carolina, Ohio, Pennsylvania, Rhode Island, and Virginia.

States with high-risk pools, however, can have waiting periods as long as a year before preexisting conditions are covered. These waiting periods can sometimes be reduced if you have had prior coverage. The Web site of Affinity Group Underwriters (www.agu.net) has some of the best and most current information on high-risk pools in the states that offer them. From the home page, click on "Industry Links." Then scroll down to "HIPAA Related Links" and click on "State Risk Pools." There you will find direct links to each state's high-risk-pool Web site if the state maintains one. Finally, if you can't get insurance of any kind in your state, you should probably consider moving to a state where you can purchase coverage or where a high-risk pool is available, since serious health-care reform is at least a decade away.

Figure 5

Where You Live Matters

Guaranteed-issue states
Insurance is guaranteed even if you have preexisting conditions, but premiums overall are usually higher. These states also use community rating, which means your premium is not based on your health.

High-risk-pool states
Insurance is not guaranteed, and those individuals with preexisting conditions who cannot get insurance can apply for coverage through the high-risk pool, usually at a higher premium cost.

No high-risk pool
No or very few insurance options for those excluded from coverage by preexisting conditions.

COVERAGE FOR COLLEGE AND UNIVERSITY STUDENTS

In my first book, *Retire on Less Than You Think: The New York Times Guide to Planning Your Financial Future,* which was published in 2004, I urged retirees who weren't sixty-five and had no retiree health benefits to enroll as college students because they would be guaranteed the right to buy student insurance. Some insurance company executives must have read the book, because insurers have recently started limiting the age of those who can buy student insurance to thirty years.

But student insurance is still important. If you're a college student and not covered by your parents' policy, you will need to arrange for your own coverage. (A small but growing number of states are forcing insurers to raise the dependent age limit on family policies from twenty-two or twenty-three to twenty-five, and in some cases thirty.) Most colleges and universities offer some kind of group health insurance that students may purchase. In addition, you can buy individual student coverage on your own through the private market and brokers like eHealthInsurance. In fact, the second choice may be the best bet.

At Kansas State University in Manhattan, Kansas, where I teach, and at other state universities in Kansas, the state offers students coverage through a plan underwritten by MEGA Life and Health Insurance Company. The plan must accept all students, regardless of any preexisting conditions, but there is a twelve-month waiting period before the insurance covers these conditions. For an individual, the deductible is only $500 a year, but the coverage is relatively meager. The maximum payment for a hospital room, for instance, is just $300 a day. There are various copayments and coinsurance charges. The maximum benefits per policy year are capped at $100,000, although students may opt to buy "major medical" coverage that lifts that to $200,000. Students must purchase the major medical option in order for chemotherapy and radiation therapy to be covered. When a student graduates or leaves school, that's it. The policy ends and is not convertible to individual coverage. For a single student, the annual premium is $1,164.50, which works out to about $97 a month.

A Kansas student going to the individual market could buy his or her coverage and get a better deal. There is, however, no guaranteed acceptance. (If you don't qualify for coverage because of preexisting conditions, there's always the university plan to fall back on. Just be careful of any time limitations for applying.) For a twenty-year-old student, the Time Insurance company offers a policy with a $500 deductible for $1,071 a year, or about $89 a month; that's $93.50 cheaper per year, or $8 a month, than the MEGA Life and Health policy. While the Time policy also won't pay for preexisting conditions for twelve months, it does have a lifetime maximum benefit of $1 million—a tenfold inprovement. There is a 20 percent coinsurance payment required for most services after the deductible has been met, but total out-of-pocket expenses are capped at $2,500 a year. There are no specific dollar limits on such things as hospital room charges. But the best part of this policy may be that you can keep it until you are thirty years old even if you drop out of school or graduate, as long as you were a full-time student for at least thirty-one days after the policy's effective date. This can be especially valuable if there is a gap between graduation and work or if your first employer out of college doesn't provide health coverage.

You can easily check out student insurance in your own state through the Web and compare it with what your college or university offers.

DISCOUNT CLUBS

In the end, if you can't get any insurance, you might be able to at least cut some of your medical bills by joining a discount club whose participants—doctors, dentists, pharmacists, even hospitals—have agreed to give members discounts from 10 to 60 percent. These clubs, however, are no substitute for health insurance. They can cost anywhere from a few dollars a month up to $75—as much as some insurance policies. There are no guarantees for the benefits, you usually have to pay cash at the time of services, and providers can drop out of the club without notice. Three better-known companies that offer discount cards are eHealthInsurance (dental cards only), Careington (www.careington.com), and AmeriPlan USA (www.ameriplanusa.com). Careington's membership runs from $11.95 a month for a dental and vision care discount card to $29.95 a month for a wider range of medical-provider discounts, including from hospitals.

Be careful that providers in your area accept the discount card. Regional coverage can be spotty. Usually, the only benefit to providers for accepting one of these discount cards is access to new patients who pay cash, which eliminates the expenses of filing insurance claims as well as delays in payments. In addition, sometimes the discount may not be much more than a provider has to give an insurance company anyway if you had insurance instead of a discount card, and you are responsible for paying the balance. It's not health insurance—be leery of fly-by-night companies promoting their cards as inexpensive "health care" or "health insurance"—but it can be better than nothing.

THE HEALTHFULNESS OF YOUR STATE

Not only does the state in which you live determine the kind of insurance you have, or whether you can get insurance at all, but where you live can also have direct consequences on your health. The United Health Foundation, a nonprofit group based in Minnetonka, Minnesota, each year ranks the states according to various health measures, including cardiovascular deaths, premature death rates, infant mortality, prevalence of smoking and obesity, per-capita health spending, and the like. For 2005, Minnesota ranked best, a position it has held for ten of the last sixteen years. Here is the foundation's ranking of all fifty states, in descending order of healthfulness:

1. Minnesota
2. Vermont
3. New Hampshire

4. Utah

5. Hawaii

6. North Dakota

7. Connecticut

8. Maine

9. Massachusetts

10. Iowa

11. Nebraska

12. Rhode Island

13. Wisconsin

14. Washington

15. New Jersey

16. Idaho

17. Colorado

18. Oregon

19. Wyoming

20. South Dakota

21. Montana

22. California

23. Kansas

24. Virginia

25. Pennsylvania

26. New York

27. Ohio

28. Illinois

29. Michigan

30. Alaska

31. Arizona

32. Indiana

33. Delaware

34. Maryland

35. Missouri

36. North Carolina

37. Nevada
38. New Mexico
39. Texas
40. Florida
41. West Virginia
42. Kentucky
43. Georgia
44. Oklahoma
45. Alabama
46. South Carolina
47. Arkansas
48. Tennessee
49. Louisiana
50. Mississippi

ONE WOMAN'S STORY

In 2001, Jeanine Caraway, then fifty-one, was working in Dallas for the Haggar Corporation, a big clothing company that provided good health insurance for its employees. She had previously worked for a catalog company in Idaho and had taught at universities in Illinois and Texas, including her alma mater, Tarleton State University. Those employers had also provided her with group health insurance. Caraway, like most Americans, didn't give much thought to health insurance because it automatically came with her jobs.

All that changed in 2001. Caraway decided to return to her native Texas to help run her family's 1,722-acre cattle ranch in Strawn, about seventy-five miles west of Fort Worth. "You know the stories you hear about executives who are burned out and have to have time off?" she said. "Well, I was one of those."

That decision forced her to confront the problem of health insurance. Thanks to COBRA, she had eighteen months to research her options. She paid $250 a month under COBRA for the same insurance she had had with Haggar. "I started looking around for private health insurance," she recalled. "I was looking for coverage close to what I had under COBRA at a price I could afford." At that time she was not aware of her rights under HIPAA; its guaranteed coverage, however, might have carried a higher premium than she wanted—as might have the state's high-risk pool, which she also didn't consider.

She finally decided to go the association route. She joined the National Association of the Self-Employed, where she found the coverage the group made available to its members through MEGA Life and Health Insurance was a bit less expensive than she could get in the individual market. Like most association policies these days, however, the coverage was not automatic. "I was concerned that I might be rejected because I suffer from hypertension, which is controlled by medication," she said. "I had to go through an extended medical interview with the insurance company, plus my doctor had to answer a questionnaire and write a letter on my behalf. I was so concerned that they might turn me down over my hypertension that I wasn't paying close attention to the other health questions. I got the insurance, but with an exclusion for anything relating to my allergies—forever. But not a word about my hypertension. I guess it was because I had had sinus surgery in the past."

When her policy was issued in 2002, the monthly premium was $260.50. Although she has never filed a claim under the policy, her premium has increased steadily. For 2006, it stood at $429.35 a month. The policy has a $3,000 annual deductible and a lifetime maximum benefit of $1 million. All medical problems, except for allergies, are covered.

Caraway, who also works part-time as a "landman" researching titles for oil leases, says she sometimes thinks she's wasting her money on health premiums. "But then I realize that I'm protecting myself against a financial catastrophe if I have a major medical problem," she added. "I view it as protection for the ranch. I could never be without health insurance."

She continued: "When I decided to become self-employed, the number one concern I had was what would happen to my health insurance. It was not whether I could make a living or would be happy. At one point when my COBRA was running out, I began to consider that I might have to go back working for a company to have health insurance. I also considered the same thing at my last premium increase.

"But the one thing I never considered was going without it. I am terrified of being without health insurance. I have seen too many people without coverage who are tempting fate. I know lots of people in that wasteland between the ages of fifty and sixty-five who have no health insurance and are waiting for Medicare, hoping nothing happens."

USING AN INSURANCE AGENT

If, after reading through all these issues, you're more comfortable dealing with an insurance agent in your area, there are three organizations with Web sites that can help you find one:

- The National Association of Health Underwriters
  (www.nahu.org)
- The Association of Health Insurance Advisors
  (www.ahia.net)
- Independent Insurance Agents and Brokers of America
  (www.iiaa.org)

6

Rx for Your Wallet

I could be charging more, but I wouldn't feel right about it.

—JIM WITT, PHARMACIST

In November 2005, the *CBS Evening News* profiled Jim Witt, a pharmacist in Ashby, Minnesota, who sells prescription drugs, especially generic ones, at prices far below what others are charging. The report mentioned the case of a woman who could not afford the $800 her prescriptions were costing her each month. Then she heard about Witt and his tiny pharmacy—there are only five hundred people in rural Ashby, which is located in the central part of Minnesota—and discovered that she could get the same drugs from him for just $200.

Intrigued, I telephoned Witt to find out more. I discovered that the woman's savings were not unusual, although the soft-spoken Witt and his pharmacy—called Borg Drug, after the original owner— certainly are. As CBS pointed out, Witt is almost single-handedly taking on the pharmaceutical industry.

Ignoring the drug companies' suggested retail price for their products, Witt is selling prescription drugs at prices that are very close to the wholesale prices he pays. For generic drugs, where a pharmacy's profit markup can be enormous, the difference is huge. CBS cited one generic drug that wholesales for around $15 and that its maker suggests should retail for $198, an astonishing increase of 1,220 percent. The markup is less significant for many brand-name drugs; drug manufacturers set the wholesale cost much higher, partly to recoup research and development expenses for new pharmaceuticals while the patent on a drug still gives them a monopoly on the market. "Pharmacies can make a lot more money percentage-wise on generic drugs," Witt explained, "but since the generics' profit margins are higher, it's where a pharmacy can save customers money."

Here's an example. Witt says his wholesale price for a thirty-day supply of 10-milligram tablets of lisinopril—a drug used to treat high blood pressure better known by its brand name Zestril—is $1.59. The suggested retail price is $29.53, an increase of 1,757 percent! Witt charges $4.86, a markup that allows him to cover some staff expenses and items like labels and vials. Many pharmacies sell drugs for less than the suggested retail price, but few match Borg Drug.

Costco, one of the least expensive places to buy drugs in the United States, charges $6.79 for the same supply of lisinopril. Few other independent pharmacies discount to Witt's level. One pharmacy in Kansas charges $23.80 for the lisinopril, and another in New Jersey charges $12.05.

For the brand-name drugs, Witt has less wiggle room to provide deep discounts of the suggested retail prices. For instance, a thirty-day supply of 20-milligram Lipitor tablets—a drug used to treat high cholesterol—costs Witt $93.63. He sells them for $96.90—the same $3.27 markup he adds to the wholesale costs of lisinopril—rather than the suggested retail price of $118.10. Witt's price is cheaper even than Costco's: The warehouse chain charges $98.57 for the same supply of Lipitor. "It works out to be pretty consistent," Witt said. "We end up being a few dollars cheaper on brand-name drugs, but we can really save people money on generic drugs. It depends on where customers have been going before."

Witt keeps the retail prices as close to wholesale as possible. "It's very tight," he said. "The pharmacy part of my business right now is essentially nonprofit. We make money on nonprescription items that are sold in the store, but that's not really significant. In a town of five hundred people, there's not a lot of walk-in business for things like that."

His hope is that as people hear about his prices, he can make money through volume. He may be on to something. He said he had been "pretty much overwhelmed" with calls from all over the country since the CBS segment was broadcast. Now, more than half his drug business is from outside of Minnesota and his area. His most distant customer lives in Hawaii. To handle the business, Witt hired more staff and installed an extra telephone line and a voice-mail system. His wife, Shannon, also helps out. Customers mail him their prescriptions, and he sends the drugs by first-class mail. Witt's Web site (www.borgdrug.com) contains directions for contacting his pharmacy and getting prescriptions filled, as well as a list of his drug prices.

Witt, who bought Borg Drug in 1999 in order to live and work closer to his family, said he had not been pressured by the pharmaceutical companies or by nearby competitors over his prices. "The drug companies don't care what I charge, as long as I pay their wholesale prices," he explained. "Other pharmacists haven't said anything, at least to my face. I think they're kind of waiting to see what happens."

It was his move to Ashby that prompted Witt to cut drug prices. "In a town this small, you get to know everybody," he said. "It's really hard to ask an older person to pay a high markup on a drug when you know they're struggling to buy food or pay rent. I just didn't feel comfortable with it. I could be charging more, but I wouldn't feel right about it. Then I thought, if it's the right thing to do for people I know, it should be the right thing to do for people I don't know." Witt goes further on the Borg Drug Web site: "I only wish that other pharmacies, drug manufacturers, and corporate America would have this same philosophy."

THE HIGH—AND SOMETIMES WEIRD—PRICES OF PRESCRIPTION DRUGS

It's pretty clear from the price comparisons above that there is an Alice-in-Wonderland quality to the all-over-the-place retail prices for prescription drugs. Sometimes they seem positively loopy. More surprising: A stronger dose of a particular drug can be almost the same price, even occasionally cheaper, than a weaker dose. If you have to pay the entire bill for your prescription drugs, finding deals can be an exercise in contortion—but because the system is so confused, there are great deals to be found.

Even if you have coverage for prescription drugs, it's important to pay attention to prices. Gone are the days when most people with drug coverage forked over a flat copay of $3 or $5 for a prescription. Copayments are rising dramatically or being replaced with coinsurance coverage, in which patients pay a percentage of a drug's cost instead of a flat per-prescription amount. That coinsurance can be 20 percent, 50 percent, or more. According to the *Wall Street Journal*, state workers in Georgia face $100 copays for certain brand-name drugs. Sometimes insurers won't pay for expensive drugs unless the prescribing doctor gets specific permission or a less expensive medication has been tried first.

Employers are cutting back on drug coverage because prices, especially for drugs often prescribed to older people, have been soaring far beyond the rate of inflation. According to the AARP, wholesale prices for the two hundred brand-name drugs most commonly used by Americans over age fifty increased an average of 6.1 percent for the twelve months ending in June 2005, about double the rate of inflation. The jump followed similar increases in the previous two years. A 2003 study by Families USA showed price increases for specific brand-name drugs ranging from two to thirteen times the Consumer Price Index. Families USA also pointed out that drug prices increase frequently, sometimes two or three times a year. A cynic might be excused for wondering if the steady rise in prices for drugs taken mainly by older people is linked to the Medicare prescription drug benefit that passed in 2003 and went into effect in 2006. Under the program, called Part D, Congress prohibited Medicare from using its buying clout to negotiate lower prices. Drug companies can charge whatever they think the market will bear or whatever they negotiate with insurance companies offering coverage under Part D. Of course, only people age sixty-five and older, or those who are disabled, qualify for Medicare, and those who do will have to negotiate gaps in coverage (see chapter 8).

Prices also seem to have little connection to the dosage prescribed. Take, for example, Lipitor, the high-cholesterol drug, which, according to the U.S. Agency for Healthcare Research and Quality, is the most prescribed drug in America, with sales of more than $7 billion a year. Pfizer's suggested retail price for a thirty-day supply (usual dose: one a day) of 20-milligram pills is $118.10. Remember that Jim Witt, the pharmacist at Borg Drug in Minnesota, pays $93.63 for a thirty-day supply; he sells it for $96.90. Costco sells the same supply of Lipitor for $98.57. Lipitor is available in strengths of 10, 20, 40, and 80 milligrams. Here's where the pricing gets weird: While Borg Drug sells thirty of the weaker 10-milligram tablets for $67.80 (Costco charges $71.47), the prices of the 20-, 40-, and 80-milligram tablets are identical, and the prices at Costco for the three higher doses vary by only about $2—meaning that the wholesale prices are most likely about the same. How can that be? Prices are even stranger at the big online retailer Drugstore.com: A thirty-day supply of 10-milligram Lipitor tablets is $68.59, but the 80-milligram supply is *cheaper*—than the 40-milligram supply at $98.99

and the 20-milligram supply at $99.99. I telephoned Drugstore.com and asked why. Here's the answer I was given: "We were able to negotiate a better price, I guess. It's all an issue of what our buying team has put together. If there were more demand for a certain dose of a drug, it would be cheaper. But the twenty milligrams of Lipitor is the most popular dose, so I'm not sure why the price is coming up that way."

High drug prices—especially for brand-name drugs—are a strain on consumers. For people without prescription coverage, they can even be financially devastating. There are, however, four easy and effective methods for lowering the cost of prescription drugs:

- Shop around and compare prices.
- Buy stronger doses and split drugs, when possible.
- Order brand-name drugs from Canada, where prices are lower.
- Consider a prescription discount card.

The first two strategies help to lower costs whether you have prescription coverage or not. Discount cards usually don't work in conjunction with insurance, but they can sometimes be used in conjunction with high-deductible policies.

COMPARING PRICES

When comparing prices on your prescriptions, check first to see if your brand-name drug has one or more generic equivalent. Many doctors automatically write prescriptions for brand-name drugs, assuming that a patient's pharmacy will substitute a generic when possible. Usually—but not always—big drug chains offer the best retail prices simply because of the huge volume of business they do. Among the chains, Costco's pharmacies almost always stand out as having the lowest prices. A 2003 survey conducted by the *Miami Herald* found Costco to be cheaper—sometimes dramatically so—for generic drugs than its competitors in South Florida; one big pharmacy charged *ten times* Costco's price for the same drug. Costco executives told the *Herald* that the price variations could be attributed to the company's policy of limiting price markups above its own wholesale prices, as compared with some of their competitors, which instead calculate their discount prices as a percentage *markdown* from the cost of a drug's brand-name equivalent. Costco charges an annual membership fee to shop at its stores, but not for use of its pharmacies. Just explain at the door that you're a pharmacy-only customer.

Let's compare some prices on a few popular brand-name and generic drugs. Figure 6 gives the retail prices for five top-selling brand-name drugs at Borg Drug (www.borgdrug.com) in Minnesota; Costco (www.costco.com); CVS (www.cvs.com); Drugstore.com

Figure 6

Price-Hunting for Brand-Name Drugs

Retailer	Lipitor (20 mg) For high cholesterol	Zocor (20 mg) For high cholesterol	Prevacid (30 mg) For stomach acid	Nexium (40 mg) For stomach acid	Zoloft (50 mg) For depression
Borg Drug	$ 96.90	$126.29	$125.37	$124.44	$ 75.02
Costco	98.57	131.29	127.27	126.37	76.57
CVS	116.99	146.99	149.99	146.99	90.99
Drugstore.com	99.99	135.99	123.99	123.99	75.99
Walgreens	109.99	139.99	145.99	139.99	86.99
Wal-Mart:					
Store	110.73	156.78	122.64	145.68	94.62
Mail-order	99.52	120.69	132.42	128.36	76.62

(www.drugstore.com); Walgreens (www.walgreens.com); and Wal-Mart (www.walmart.com). Figure 7 shows the prices at the same concerns for five top-selling generic drugs. All prices are for a thirty-day supply of the most commonly prescribed strengths. (Where a Web site provided prices based on a larger or smaller supply, I calculated and listed the thirty-day price equivalent.) By the time this book is published, many prices likely will have changed, but the relative differences should remain fairly constant. All but Wal-Mart's prices are available online. In the case of Wal-Mart, I give both its store prices and its mail-order prices, which can be quite different. Store prices also vary around the country, depending on competition and other local factors; the store prices used here are from two Wal-Mart stores in Kansas; the mail-order prices were obtained over the phone.

As these two charts make clear, it pays to shop around for your prescriptions. For example, the price for Lipitor ranged from a low of $96.90 at Borg Drug to a high of $116.99 at CVS, a difference of 20 percent. Interestingly, Zocor, which also lowers cholesterol, had a low of $120.69 at Wal-Mart's mail-order business and a high of $156.78 at the sample Wal-Mart store, a 30 percent difference from the same retailer.

When we consider the price differences for the generic drugs, things really get interesting. Lisinopril, the blood pressure drug, sold for a $5.99 low at Borg Drug (for 20-milligram tablets; Borg's price of $4.86 in an earlier example was for 10-milligram tablets) and a $20.70 high at the sample Wal-Mart store, a more than threefold difference! Atenolol, prescribed to regulate heartbeat and control blood pressure, ran from $3.02 at Wal-Mart (mail order) to $8.62 at Wal-Mart (store), a split of 185 percent. Amoxicillin, an antibiotic, went from $4.49 at Borg Drug to $11.99 at Walgreens, a 167 percent difference. There is no better evidence for the through-the-looking-glass quality of drug pricing than the fact that two different operations of the same company, Wal-Mart, have both the lowest *and* the highest

Figure 7

Price-Hunting for Generic Drugs

Retailer	Lisinopril (20 mg) For high blood pressure	Atenolol (50 mg) For heart-beat, blood pressure	Amoxicillin (250 mg) Antibiotic	Hydrochlo-rothiazide (50 mg) For high blood pressure	Furo-semide (20 mg) For high blood pressure
Borg Drug	$ 5.99	$ 4.25	$ 4.49	$ 4.76	$ 3.83
Costco	6.29	3.79	6.39	5.49	4.39
CVS	13.69	5.40	10.99	3.90	5.70
Drugstore.com	10.39	3.66	7.99	2.70	2.70
Walgreens	18.50	6.00	11.99	4.50	3.00
Wal-Mart:					
Store	20.70	8.62	7.36	7.88	5.78
Mail-order	10.44	3.02	5.63	3.69	2.79

prices for the brand-name drug Zocor, as well as atenolol, a generic drug. Go figure.

You must also consider shipping charges when comparing prices of your drugs. Such charges, however, are usually relatively modest and are not pegged to order size. So if you have several prescriptions to fill, shipping costs will be a very small additional charge on top of each drug's price. Some companies advertise free shipping, but check first because there can be exceptions.

Overall, Borg Drug and Costco tend to have the best prices. Borg, a small pharmacy, offers more personal service, while Costco's Web site is informative and easy to navigate. Because prices vary so much, it's probably worth setting up an account at several companies in order to take advantage of their different price breaks. Calling most of the big companies through the toll-free numbers listed on their Web sites is the usual trip through a voice-mail jungle, but setting up an account is relatively simple with a credit card. Once you have an account, getting price quotes and placing orders usually runs smoothly. If you don't have access to the Internet, here are the phone numbers for the companies we have discussed, although the numbers are subject to change:

Borg Drug	218-747-2988
Costco	800-955-2292
CVS	888-607-4287
Drugstore.com	800-378-4786
Walgreens	800-999-2655
Wal-Mart (mail order)	800-966-6546

SPLITTING PILLS

The fact is, because of the quirky way drugs are priced, many pills cost pretty much the same regardless of the dosage. That's why pill-splitting can be a great strategy for cutting the cost of a drug in half. For example, if your doctor prescribes 20 milligrams of Lipitor, your best price is $96.90 a month. But the 40-milligram tablets would also cost the same $96.90 and can be cut in half to last twice as long—saving you 50 percent. You will have to get your doctor to agree to the plan, of course.

As it happens, some insurance companies are now urging their clients to practice pill-splitting and even offering pill-splitting devices to make the job easier, according to a November 2005 article in the *Wall Street Journal.* The easiest pills to cut are those that are flat, round, and scored down the center—that is, obviously designed to be halved. Pill-splitting works only if a pill comes in double your needed dose. Pill-cutting devices won't cut pills into thirds, and cutting pills into fourths can be tricky, altering your dosage day to day. Odd-shaped pills are more difficult; you can find more expensive devices that make cutting irregularly shaped pills like Viagra a snap.

Prices for pill-cutters range from $3 at your local drugstore to as much as $25 online for a more versatile model. (Just put "pill-splitter" into an Internet search engine like Google for options. Or you can go directly to a site like www.seniorshops.com.)

Capsules with powder or gel inside obviously can't be split. And some medicines, like extended-relief tablets or certain migraine drugs, should not be cut because they work as their various layers dissolve in your stomach. Splitting them interferes with that process.

Drug makers and many pharmacists have long argued that pill-splitting is risky because patients may create irregular doses or may attempt it with inappropriate drugs. But the *Wall Street Journal* article pointed out that "a slew of research demonstrates that for many medications, pill-splitting is entirely safe when done correctly." The article cites a June 2005 report in the *American Journal of Cardiology* that examined voluntary pill-splitting of cholesterol drugs among nearly four thousand patients at six Veterans Affairs centers in Florida. There was no difference in outcome between splitters and nonsplitters. Further, pill-splitting saved the VA more than $46 million in 2003.

As it turns out, pill-splitting may be necessary even if you're not trying to save money. I take a prescription drug that only comes in 300-milligram tablets. I used to take one a day, but my doctor increased my dosage to 450 milligrams a day. His instructions: Cut the pills in half to get the required strength.

So if you want to save on prescriptions, check to see if the drug or drugs you take come in a strength that is double what you're currently prescribed. Then consult with your doctor and make sure the pills are available in a form that can be safely split. (Don't assume that the version you are taking is the only form the pills come in.) Your doctor can then write the prescription for your double dose.

An unanswered question is how long drug makers will continue selling different strengths of drugs at basically the same price once pill-splitting catches on in a big way. This is an especially relevant question now that insurance companies are encouraging patients to take up the practice. After all, it's an odd business model that allows customers to reduce the price of a product by 50 percent. If the pharmaceutical companies do decide to change their pricing to reflect a drug's strength, maybe they would lower the price of the weaker doses instead of raising the price of the stronger ones. I wouldn't bet on it, though.

BUYING DRUGS FROM CANADA

If you need to track down even more savings, particularly on brand-name drugs, look north of the border. Drugs in Canada are cheaper because the government controls the prices. Americans who buy brand-name drugs from Canadian pharmacies save significant amounts of money. But the practice has some potential pitfalls. It depends on the willingness of the Canadian government to allow its country to be a backdoor pharmacy for America; it also flies in the face of some U.S. laws and faces growing pressure from the pharmaceutical industry. Nonetheless, states are getting in on the act, whether encouraging residents to buy cheaper drugs from Canada or importing them directly for groups such as state workers, even against fierce opposition from drug makers. One exception: In December 2005, the Texas attorney general struck down a new state law intended to help the state's residents buy less expensive drugs from Canada, ruling that it violated federal law. For now, though, you can take advantage of our friendly neighbors to the north, and thanks to the Internet, you don't have to take a bus to Winnipeg to save money on your prescriptions.

How much money? A lot. Figure 8 shows the prices of the top five brand-name drugs for Canada Pharmacy (www.canadapharmacy. com), which is based in Surrey, British Columbia, and offers only

Figure 8

Saving on Brand-Name Drugs from Canada

	Lipitor (20 mg) For high cholesterol	Zocor (20 mg) For high cholesterol	Prevacid (30 mg) For stomach acid	Nexium (40 mg) For stomach acid	Zoloft (50 mg) For depression
Lowest U.S. price*	$96.90	$120.69	$122.64	$123.99	$75.02
Canada Pharmacy	58.33	62.40	87.00	87.86	61.50

Lowest price of retailers surveyed in Figure 6.

telephone and Internet service. A thirty-day supply of 20-milligram Lipitor tablets from Canada Pharmacy costs $58.33, a 40 percent savings from the lowest U.S. price at Borg Drug. Drugs from Canada are often available only in ninety-day and one-hundred-day supplies, but I adjusted the prices so they could be compared with costs for a thirty-day supply from the cheapest U.S. outlet (see figure 6).

If you're willing to split pills, the savings can even be greater. For a thirty-day supply of 40-milligram Lipitor tablets, Canada Pharmacy charges $65, only $6.67 more than for the 20-milligram tablets. Splitting the 40-milligram tablets halves the price to $32.50 a month. That's 33 percent less than if you did the same to 40-milligram pills from Borg Drug.

While brand-name drugs are cheaper in Canada, that's not necessarily the case for generics, as figure 9 makes clear. Most generic drugs are as cheap, if not cheaper, in the United States.

I called Canada Pharmacy's toll-free number (800-891-0844) to find out some of the details involved in ordering Canadian drugs over the Internet. It turns out to be relatively easy. Representatives are available twenty-four hours a day, seven days a week, and the waiting time to speak with someone is far shorter than is typical in

Figure 9

No Deals on Generic Drugs from Canada

	Lisinopril (20 mg)	Atenolol (50 mg)	Amoxicillin (250 mg)	Hydrochlorothiazide (50 mg)	Furosemide (20 mg)
	For high blood pressure	For heartbeat, blood pressure	Antibiotic	For high blood pressure	For high blood pressure
Lowest U.S. price*	$ 5.99	$ 3.02	$ 4.49	$ 2.70	$ 2.70
Canada Pharmacy	22.50	8.70	5.70	4.20	4.50

*Lowest price of retailers surveyed in Figure 7.

the United States. To get an account started at Canada Pharmacy, you must simply fax the company a valid form of ID, such as a driver's license, passport, or birth certificate. Then you fax the prescriptions from your American doctor. The prescriptions are sent to a Canadian doctor, who confirms the specifications and writes a Canadian prescription for the drugs you need. "Regulations won't allow us to accept a U.S. prescription," according to a representative of Canada Pharmacy. "Our doctor will check with your U.S. doctor if there is something missing or wrong with your prescription." The Canadian prescription is filled and shipped via regular mail. The whole process takes two to three weeks. Refills are faster because they don't have to be routed through a Canadian doctor. The only risk is a hang-up with U.S. Customs, but the Canadian Pharmacy representative said this happens "not too often," in part because prescriptions are shipped from the company pharmacy in Surrey, as well as from a pharmacy in the United States. Obviously, prescriptions mailed from the U.S. facility would not face customs problems.

Canada Pharmacy sells just about every drug available in the United States, except controlled substances and narcotics, which cannot be shipped internationally. You can check the price for a drug, in U.S. dollars, on the company's Web site. Drugs are only dispensed in quantities listed on the site, usually in packs of ninety, so it helps if your prescriptions are written that way. But if a prescription is for less than ninety days, the pharmacy will deduct the excess out of the refills.

Shipping is $10 (U.S.) per order, regardless of the number of items. Customers can opt to pay a onetime shipping charge of $50 (U.S.) and get lifetime shipping for everyone listed on the account. You can pay for your prescriptions by credit card, electronic check, or money order. If you agree to undergo a quick credit check, you can open an account and be billed through a third-party billing agency if you don't want to use a credit card or bother with electronic checks or money orders.

BUYING DRUGS FROM MEXICO

I have reservations about buying drugs in Mexico, mainly because of the risk of getting fake or substandard medicines. According to research cited by the Center for Pharmacoeconomic Studies at the University of Texas at Austin, one in five drugs from Mexico is counterfeit or substandard. Another problem is that many drugs in Mexico are available without a prescription, which can be an invitation to self-medication and dangerous drug interactions. Various brands of some drugs, whose active ingredients are chemically the same, but which include different inactive ingredients, can also create problems for some people.

However, thousands of Americans who live along the Mexican border routinely travel to Mexico to buy drugs at much cheaper prices than in the United States. There are Mexican pharmacies that cater to Americans at almost every border town. When traveling from Mexico to the United States with prescription drugs, you must declare them. You're usually allowed to bring in a supply of three months or less. For some drugs, you may need to show a prescription to carry the drugs into the United States. Consult U.S. Customs officials before buying.

It's also possible to get drugs through the mail from Mexico, but the practice is not as common as it is with Canadian pharmacies. If you're interested in checking out this option, a good place to start is www.MedBasketMexico.com.

PRESCRIPTION DISCOUNT CARDS

In chapter 5, we looked at the savings generally available from discount clubs and discount cards. For a monthly membership fee, you receive a discount at participating pharmacies. The membership fees and discounts vary, but these cards can save you money if you have no prescription coverage or have a health insurance policy with a high deductible under which you must pay the full price for your prescriptions and submit the receipts for reimbursement only after you have met your deductible. You generally cannot use discount cards in conjunction with prescription coverage that requires only a copayment. No matter what discount club you join, you will not beat the savings on brand-name drugs that you will get by filling your prescriptions in Canada. In fact, discount cards can often give you the biggest savings on generic drugs since their markups are much greater than for brand-name drugs. Just remember: Discount cards are not insurance; they just offer a possible discount off the retail price.

One pharmacist I talked with said he accepted several of these cards because he found it "very difficult to turn away people who need prescriptions." The companies that issue the discount cards do not reimburse him. In fact, sometimes he has to pay them a small fee for each prescription he fills. "What's in it for me is a customer," he said. "If another pharmacy doesn't accept the card, I get the patient."

Many discount cards are offered through big retail stores, others on the Internet. Three of these discount cards and their Web sites are listed, along with more details, in chapter 5. Check that there are pharmacies in your area that accept the particular card you are considering. Ask your pharmacist which cards he or she accepts or recommends and what specific discounts are available on the drugs you take.

To stretch your medical dollars even further, combine a prescription discount card with pill-splitting when possible.

MEDICARE PART D

Prescription coverage for Medicare beneficiaries went into effect at the beginning of 2006. The launch of the benefit, called Medicare Part D, was accompanied by much angst and confusion on the part of people over age sixty-five—and no wonder: It is one of the worst pieces of legislation ever passed by Congress. It is maddeningly complex, inconsistent, encourages high drug prices, has enormous coverage gaps, and, because it is voluntary, invites adverse selection, ensuring that its costs will increase since the people with the biggest drug bills are far more likely to enroll. It had so many start-up problems in its first month that many states had to step in with emergency help. Saul Friedman, a columnist for *Newsday,* perhaps best expressed the frustrations over Medicare Part D: "First, the new law was more a gift to the insurance and drug industries than it was a benefit for Medicare enrollees, because most of the estimated $720 billion spent under the new law will go to those industries. Furthermore, the law undermines Medicare as a government health program by requiring enrollees to buy private insurance in which Medicare plays no role. And for the first time, the Medicare principle of universality was lost when a means test was instituted for low-income beneficiaries." Indeed, if the plan were mandatory for everyone eligible for Medicare, it would be partially subsidized by premiums from individuals who need fewer prescriptions.

Because many insurance companies offer so many permutations of the plan, it is extremely confusing. In forty-six states, Medicare beneficiaries can currently choose from forty or more plans, according to the Kaiser Family Foundation. In Texas, for instance, twenty insurance companies offer forty-seven different drug plans. Because different plans have different formularies, or lists of drugs that are covered, as well as varying copays and deductibles, it is very difficult to compare them. You must be careful that the drugs you take are on the formulary of the plan you sign up for. Copays are supposed to be 25 percent of a drug's price and the annual deductible is supposed to be around $250, but insurance companies have wide latitude to vary both. Premiums are all over the place, ranging from as low as $1.87 a month to a high of $99.90. According to the federal Centers for Medicare and Medicaid Services, the average premium is about $32.

For those with retiree health benefits, including prescription coverage, from their former employers, there is a special danger. If you decide to try Medicare Part D instead of your retiree drug coverage, you may lose all of your retiree medical benefits. In other words, stay put—or lose everything. That's because some companies say they can't separate drug coverage from a package of health benefits. There are other companies, however, that have no trouble separating the coverage; they now unceremoniously dump retirees from drug coverage when they hit age sixty-five, suggesting they sign up for the Medicare Part D instead.

Famously, Part D is also riddled with gaps in coverage. Here, instead of going down a rabbit hole, you fall through the "doughnut hole." First, you must meet the annual deductible of $250; after that there are copayments of 25 percent for each prescription, depending on your plan. So far, so good. But if your cumulative drug expenses reach $2,250, you're suddenly on your own. The Medicare drug benefit disappears until your costs hit $5,100—leaving you on the hook for $2,850. Paul Krugman of the *New York Times* pointed out the bizarre effect of this doughnut hole: If you are a retiree and spend $2,000 a year on drugs, Medicare will cover about 66 percent of your expenses. If, however, you spend $5,000—and presumably are more likely to need help paying those bills—Medicare will pay only about 30 percent of your prescription expenses. This, Krugman says, will put people with continuing high drug expenses on a financial roller-coaster ride that will repeat itself year after year.

Supplemental insurance might have been used to cover the gap, but such insurance is specifically prohibited under the 2003 legislation that created the Part D benefit. The prohibition was put in place in deference to the "moral hazard" conundrum. Congress figured private hole-filling coverage, even if you pay for it, might cause you to ask your doctor for drugs you don't really need. A report accompanying the final Medicare prescription bill when it was passed in 2003 specifically called upon the moral hazard argument when it said that the purpose of the insurance prohibition was to keep beneficiaries from becoming "insensitive to costs." Well, if you or your mother needs a prescription, "sensitivity" is not going to lessen your or your mother's ability to buy it. Why should people not be allowed to buy private insurance to augment this government program? By that logic, we should limit comprehensive auto insurance to make people sensitive to high repair costs. Deane Beebe, a spokeswoman for the Medicare Rights Center, the nonprofit group based in New York that helps people handle Medicare and Medicare HMO/PPO problems, said of the insurance prohibition: "The whole concept is based on the idea that people will use too much medication if they have coverage. We're really troubled by that." The piece of legislation that created Part D is, on the other hand, not at all sensitive to the pharmaceutical industry's prices. It prohibits Medicare from using its buying clout—as does, for example, the Veterans Administration—to negotiate lower drug costs.

Some big insurers, including Humana (www.humana.com), are able to offer coverage for the doughnut hole, and sometimes part of the deductible, in their most expensive policies because they can negotiate such good prices with drug makers that they don't end up spending any more money, which they are not allowed to do, to cover this gap. Although prices vary depending on where you live, Humana's policies that cover the $2,850 doughnut hole can be ten times as expensive as its cheapest policy. Copays can be as much as $30 for a single prescription of a "preferred" brand-name drug and as much as $60 for a "nonpreferred" brand-name drug, depending on your total annual drug bill. For example, in Essex County, New Jersey, Humana's basic policy is $4.43 a month; the most expensive, covering the doughnut hole, is $48.50. Of course, the price might be worth it if you have big drug bills. You can check the details on policies for your area on Humana's Web site.

Yet most Medicare Part D policies don't cover the doughnut hole, and you cannot buy supplemental coverage to cover it. One other option: If you expect to hit the doughnut hole, but also expect to fall short of spending the $5,100 necessary to emerge from it, turn to a Canadian pharmacy the minute you hit the hole. Be very careful, however, because drugs purchased from a Canadian pharmacy don't count toward getting out of the hole unless that pharmacy is in your plan's network of pharmacies. The Medicare Rights Center said it knew of no Canadian pharmacies that were currently included in any plan's network.

What's the bottom line? If you turn sixty-five and are not covered by a retiree health plan that includes prescription drug benefits, or you get kicked out of your retiree plan, you probably should sign up for Part D even if you don't currently take a lot of drugs for your health care. There is a financial penalty if you delay your enrollment, and, face it, you may someday need expensive drugs—especially as more and more health care is delivered through prescriptions rather than surgery and other treatments. The Medicare coverage, inadequate as it is, is better than none. According to government and other estimates, Part D is expected to save, on average, 37 percent of a senior's out-of-pocket drug costs. AARP found that many people will pay less enrolled in Part D—depending on the plan selected and the drugs taken—than if they skipped the coverage entirely and bought their drugs from Canada.

STATE RANKINGS BY COST OF AN AVERAGE PRESCRIPTION

Not only do prescription prices vary a lot from pharmacy to pharmacy, there are also state and regional factors that affect prices. According to the Kaiser Family Foundation, in 2003, the most recent year data were available, the national average onetime cost of a single prescription was $52.97. However, the price of that prescription could run from as little as $44.71, almost 16 percent less than the average, in New Mexico, to $66.89, or about 26 percent more than the average, in Alaska. Here are the rankings and prices for all the states and Washington, D.C.

1. Alaska	$66.89
2. District of Columbia	$66.81
3. Maryland	$64.96
4. New York	$63.34
5. New Jersey	$62.20
6. Maine	$59.04
7. Delaware	$58.96
8. Michigan	$55.84
9. Alabama	$55.42
10. Washington	$54.90
11. Minnesota	$54.62
12. Pennsylvania	$54.52
13. Florida	$54.33
14. Connecticut	$54.12

15. Idaho	$53.97
16. Vermont	$53.28
17. Virginia	$53.26
18. North Carolina	$53.18
19. New Hampshire	$53.10
20. Hawaii	$52.31
21. North Dakota	$52.18
22. California	$51.94
23. Massachusetts	$51.84
24. West Virginia	$51.84
25. Louisiana	$51.81
26. Texas	$51.80
27. Utah	$51.64
28. Nevada	$51.56
29. Colorado	$51.51
30. Georgia	$51.35
31. Ohio	$51.29
32. Wyoming	$51.23
33. South Carolina	$50.83
34. Mississippi	$50.64
35. Kansas	$50.02
36. Oklahoma	$49.98
37. Montana	$49.85
38. Arizona	$49.73
39. Oregon	$49.55
40. Rhode Island	$49.39
41. Wisconsin	$49.16
42. Nebraska	$49.08
43. Indiana	$48.93
44. Tennessee	$48.75
45. Missouri	$48.58
46. Kentucky	$48.57
47. Iowa	$48.54

48. Illinois	$48.11
49. South Dakota	$47.53
50. Arkansas	$44.76
51. New Mexico	$44.71

This ranking further illustrates the importance of shopping around for the best prices, especially if you live near the border of a state with cheaper prices. The difference between Arizona and New Mexico is more than $5 per prescription; between New York and Connecticut, it's almost $10. If you live in one of the more expensive states, such as Alaska, it makes even more sense to consider buying prescriptions from Canada.

HELP FROM THE DRUG COMPANIES

If you don't have prescription drug coverage, you may be eligible for free drugs from pharmaceutical companies. Virtually all the drug makers will provide free medicines for those who have no drug coverage and whose incomes fall below certain levels. The income limits are not always that strict; in some cases, people earning as much as $60,000 a year can qualify. One unavoidable wrinkle is that you must apply separately to each company that makes your medications. The drugs are commonly dispensed through doctors, and patients usually have to requalify regularly.

Before the Medicare drug benefit became effective in 2006, Medicare beneficiaries were eligible for such free drugs. Several drug makers have since excluded elderly patients from the giveaways because they qualify for Medicare Part D—whether they sign up for it or not. But there are still some companies that dispense free drugs to those over sixty-five if they have not signed up for Part D. You can check the Web sites of companies that manufacture your prescribed drugs or the Web site of the Pharmaceutical Research and Manufacturers of America (www.phrma.org) to find out more about these programs, which are lumped together under what the trade group calls the Partnership for Prescription Assistance. If you don't have access to the Internet, you can call the Partnership for Prescription Assistance at 888-477-2669.

There are companies that, for a relatively small fee, will provide information on the various free-drug programs offered by the pharmaceutical companies, including each company's eligibility requirement. One is Harson Hill (www.prescriptions4free.com). While these services can be helpful, you really don't need to pay for this information. The Pharmaceutical Research and Manufacturers of America Web site has the same information—for free—that companies like Harson Hill are selling. Drug companies will provide information directly to doctors.

The drug companies do not heavily advertise these programs. Even some doctors are unaware of them, and others avoid the offers because of the paperwork. In reality, the paperwork is really not that difficult. Sometimes it's just one page, along with copies of your tax returns or other income documentation that you supply to your doctor. If your doctor's office resists applying for a free drug program, don't back down.

JUGGLING THE PHARMACIES

If you shop for prescription drugs solely on the basis of price, you will most likely get different prescriptions filled by different pharmacies. That can be fine if you are certain you understand the side effects of drugs you are taking and how they interact with other drugs, but if you are not sure about interactions or need help sorting it out, you may need another solution. The advantage of buying all your prescriptions from one pharmacy is that a pharmacist is able, often with the help of a computer program, to keep track of what you are taking and warn you of conflicts and problems.

One option is to find a single U.S. pharmacy that offers competitive, low prices on generic drugs and order your brand-name drugs from Canada. Explain to the pharmacist exactly what you are doing, give him or her a list of your brand-name drugs, and ask for help spotting any unfavorable interactions. Since the pharmacy's profit markup on generics is much greater than it is for brand-name drugs, most pharmacists will not have a problem providing the information to you. In fact, it is not an unusual request since pharmacies often have customers whose drug coverage plans require certain maintenance medicines to be purchased from distant mail-order companies or who get some of their drugs from the Veterans Administration.

7

Mastering Your Insurer's Fine Print

Complexity is the friend of insurance companies.

—SENATOR HILLARY RODHAM CLINTON

Richard Price, a retired equity portfolio manager in Miami Beach, Florida, learned the value of studying very carefully each explanation of benefits, or EOB, his insurance company sends him.

In reviewing his statements for 2004 and 2005, he discovered that Aetna, which provides his retiree health insurance, seemed to have underpaid him by as much as $10,000.

Price and his wife, Mary, who were both in their early sixties at the time, held a policy with an annual deductible of $500 for each of them for their in-network health services. The out-of-network deductible of $5,000 per person excluded most dental care, some mental health care, and any charges in excess of what Aetna deemed to be "reasonable and customary."

Price first began to suspect errors in Aetna's payments to him after he spent five days in the hospital in August 2005 for the treatment of diverticulitis. "I noticed that there were bills that should have been paid at one hundred percent that were being paid at seventy percent," he said.

He then began to look at his EOBs for the previous two years. "There was a pattern to the errors, which mainly stemmed from sloppy processing and dates of services being listed out of order. Sometimes they paid zero for bills they should have paid. Whenever I called, they were very polite and said, 'Oh yes, we'll fix that.' Other times bills would be duplicated. For instance, my wife and I are each allowed forty visits a year with a psychiatrist. These bills would sometimes be duplicated so that one visit actually counted as two toward the forty."

Price kept careful records, including copies and his and Mary's bills and their EOBs. "Sometimes the people at Aetna would say they didn't receive something; I always have copies ready to send them," he said. "Other times they seem unsure about what my benefits really are. But I'm persistent. Sometimes a problem is solved quickly; other times I have to go back and back. You must double-check everything yourself very carefully. If you don't catch problems yourself, you will be out the money. Period." He has already collected $3,000 of the unpaid benefits and is zeroing in on the remainder.

One of Price's biggest complaints, echoing those of Nancy Dennis, the Richmond, Virginia, woman we met in chapter 2 who suffers from the nervous system disorder, is that his insurer seems to have no institutional memory. With each call to Aetna, he had to start from scratch. "If you question twenty items and the score is eighteen to two in your favor, you would assume someone there would think, 'Gee, there must be something wrong with our system.' There seems to be no way for them to pick up on that," Price noted. "They ought to have a system to do that."

STRATEGIES FOR AVOIDING OR RESOLVING PROBLEMS WITH YOUR INSURER

Most of the mistakes by insurance companies that I have personally had to deal with over the years have almost always been in the insurer's favor, not mine. That seems to be the rule. Insurance carriers have every financial incentive to delay or underpay individual claims. It is up to you to force them to do otherwise.

The usual problems people confront over their coverage fall into four categories (discussed in detail in the following section):

- Charges that are above what your insurer says are reasonable and customary (R&C).
- Health services that your insurance company deems are not medically necessary.
- Unexpected out-of-network charges over which you have little control—often a surprise by-product of being hospitalized in an in-network hospital.
- Mistakes and delays in calculating your benefits, as in Richard Price's case.

You need to arm yourself to be able to deal with these problems or, better yet, avoid them altogether. Before you see a doctor, go to a hospital, or file a claim, you should make sure that you understand what kind of policy you have, what it covers, and what your options are. On this score, the Kaiser Family Foundation maintains a very helpful Web site (www.kff.org/consumerguide), especially if you are appealing the rejection of a claim. A checklist on the site guides you toward the information you must know about your coverage.

- Is your coverage through an individual policy or an employer?
- If through an employer, is it *insured* or *self-funded*? If it is insured, your company purchases health coverage from a commercial insurer. If self-funded (or self-insured), your employer pays your health costs directly, though it may do so through an insurance carrier that acts as a third-party administrator, paying the bills with the company's money. It's not always easy to tell which type of plan your company has; even if your company self-insures, you may receive an insurance card from a company like Aetna. If

you are not certain which kind of insurance you have, ask your company's human resources department. *It is important*: If your company is self-insured, you cannot appeal a claims decision to your state insurance regulatory agency for external review; instead, you are limited to an internal review, which could decrease your chances of reversing a decision. The Kaiser site is interactive and allows you to click on a map for details about your state's external review program. Though many states have established independent medical review boards to hear appeals, a few have not: Idaho, Mississippi, Nebraska, North Dakota, South Dakota, and Wyoming. If you live in one of those states, your fate is left entirely to your insurer.

· Is your health plan a health maintenance organization (HMO); a preferred provider organization (PPO); a point-of-service plan (POS); or a traditional indemnity plan, also known as a fee-for-service plan? The kind of plan you have determines your limitations on seeing a doctor or provider of your choice. HMOs are the most limited. If your plan is a PPO or POS, what out-of-network services are *not* covered? If you use allowed out-of-network providers, what is the annual deductible and coinsurance payment for charges exceeding the deductible?

· What services does your plan *not* pay for?

· What hospitals are included in your plan's coverage?

· What are the stipulations on paying for care if you travel outside your plan's coverage area?

I would add two questions to the Kaiser Family Foundation list:

· What are the conditions under which your insurer will pay for hospital emergency room services, even—or especially—if you are not admitted to the hospital?

· Where is the booklet that explains your plan's benefits?

Armed with the answers to these questions, you will be much better equipped to make health-provider choices that may avoid coverage rejections in the first place and the appeals process altogether. If there are rejections, you will be better able to determine if they are valid or not.

It's also a good idea to keep a log, or diary, of all the health-care providers you visit and all the services you receive, including a log during hospitalizations; a small battery-operated tape recorder can help. If you are unable to keep a hospital log yourself, ask a relative or friend to maintain it for you. Ninety percent of the hospital bills that are reviewed or challenged contain errors against the patient that are usually corrected in his or her favor. You should also keep a log of your conversations with insurance company representatives. In all cases, note the date and the time of services or conversations with providers or insurance representatives; get the name or employee number of each person you speak with; summarize in a sentence or two the service provided, the conversation, or the resolution. This may sound like a lot of work, but if you set up the logs now and get into the habit of recording information as things are happening— which takes only a few minutes—the logs could be of immense value later if you have to fight over a benefit.

It may seem obvious, but be calm, courteous, and factual when speaking with customer service representatives at your insurance company. Avoid emotional outbursts. If you have problems with someone, simply ask to speak to a supervisor. Many customer service representatives receive only modest training and may not be aware of your specific policy's benefits. If you make three or four calls to your insurer with the same question, you may get different answers from different representatives; that is a clear indication you need to ask for a supervisor. Be forceful if a representative resists putting you through to a supervisor. If you do find a customer service representative who is especially helpful and knowledgeable about your coverage, request to speak with that person in subsequent calls. You may be able to build a relationship that will prove beneficial. There may be a wait for that person to return your call if he or she is busy with other clients, but it will be worth it.

Set up a filing system to track your bills, claims, and EOBs. Some insurers will not supply another EOB if you misplace the original, so keep copies if you are sending paperwork to the insurer. In many states, when an insurance company receives a claim from you, or from your doctor or other health-care provider on your behalf, the insurer is required to respond within a set period of time, often thirty days. Unfortunately, that response can simply be a notice that your claim has been received and that more information is needed for it to be processed.

If your claim is partly or totally rejected, the insurer is required to tell you why. Insurers are also usually required to explain the appeals process to you, usually on the same form containing the rejection. Before you start an appeal, you will want to sort out the company's internal review process (even in states with review boards, all appeals must start with an appeal to your insurance company) and the deadline for appeals. Put as much as you can in writing to your insurance company, creating a paper trail that may help you later. The writing doesn't have to be fancy, just factual: names, dates, and the logical reasons you think the benefit denial should be reversed—along with any supporting documents.

FIGHTING REJECTIONS

Let's look in detail at the four main reasons people usually cite when they have coverage issues with an insurer.

Reasonable-and-customary charges: If you have an indemnity plan, or go out of network under a PPO or POS plan, you will probably be reimbursed at 70 to 80 percent of what your insurer considers to be the "reasonable-and-customary" (R&C) charges for those services in your geographic area—after your deductible has been met, of course. The rub is that the actual charges might be a lot more than the insurer's R&C, leaving you on the hook for way more than 20 or 30 percent of the bill. Let's say you undergo an operation by an out-of-network surgeon and your PPO has a $1,000 deductible for such services; after that it will pay 70 percent of the reasonable-and-customary charges. If the surgeon's bill is $5,000, you might assume the insurer would pay 70 percent of $4,000, or $2,800. Think again. Say the insurer has set its R&C for your surgery at $2,000. Subtracting the deductible leaves $1,000, of which the insurer will pay 70 percent, or $700. Suddenly you're stuck with a bill for $4,300 (including the deductible), not the $2,200 you expected (including the deductible). Even if you have already met the deductible with other services, the insurance company will pay only 70 percent of its $2,000 R&C, or $1,400—leaving you responsible for $3,600. It may seem arbitrary and unfair, but it's the way the system works.

How do insurers determine what is reasonable and customary? Well, it's sort of a secret. In 2004, the *Wall Street Journal* reported that most of the major insurance companies use data supplied by the Prevailing Healthcare Charges System, a billing database operated by Ingenix, a unit of UnitedHealth Group, the big insurer based in Minneapolis, to create "reasonable-and-customary" reimbursement tables. But, the article points out, insurers won't make these tables available to consumers, arguing that they are proprietary and that making R&C tables public would encourage doctors who charge less than the listed fees to raise their prices. The result, of course, is that patients are pretty much in the dark. One tactic for fighting back against these secret tables is to ask several doctors in your area what they charge for a service to see how the average compares with what your insurer says is reasonable and customary. If the average is considerably above what your insurance company calls reasonable and customary, it can buttress your case in an appeal.

Not Medically Necessary: If a claim is rejected as "not medically necessary," the first thing you should do is pull out your benefits booklet to see if the procedure, or something like it, is listed as covered by your policy. If the booklet's description of benefits doesn't give you a basis for an appeal, ask your doctor to write a letter to your insurance company stating that the procedure in question was necessary and explaining why. Be prepared to appeal this issue as far as possible, to an external review board if allowed. After all, what is medically necessary should be a decision made by your doctor, not a faceless bureaucrat. You may well have a strong case. According to the Kaiser Family Foundation, a 2003 study of medical-necessity appeals to Maryland's external board showed that consumers were successful about half the time.

Unexpected out-of-network charges: As demonstrated by the example of the $5,000 surgery bill, out-of-network charges, combined with reasonable-and-customary limits, can add up quickly. They can also be unexpected and extremely high when you go to an in-network hospital; you think that any charges related to your hospitalization will also be in-network, only to discover later that the emergency room physician, the anesthesiologist, the radiologist, or the consulting surgeon were out-of-network, even though you had no say in choosing these doctors. That's because hospitals don't force their doctors to belong to the hospital's insurance networks. Sometimes insurance companies will provide in-network benefits to out-of-network doctors in the case of an emergency. Otherwise, more of the bill is punted onto the patient. While there are no easy solutions to this problem, you can avoid it by planning ahead for nonemergency hospital procedures. Talk to your doctor about your insurance limitations. Are there in-network specialists that could be tapped? Most important, check your state's regulations. Some states require insurers to cover all care at in-network hospitals even if an out-of-network doctor gets involved. If necessary, appeal your claim to your insurance company and beyond, if possible.

Mistakes and delays: As you can see from Richard Price's experience, you have to keep a sharp eye out for mistakes—including double billing, improper billing, and random errors—and delays that go on too long. This means you must know your benefits, including time limits for filing claims and making appeals, and maintain a good filing system to track bills and EOBs, as well as a health-care log. Nancy Dennis, who was profiled in chapter 2, has some revealing insights into how insurance companies deal with claims. Trained as a nurse before she became ill, Dennis worked as a claims adjuster for three different insurers. She says that when insurance companies reject claims, they count on a certain percentage of their clients to simply accept that the claim has been rejected and pay the bills themselves. "In my experience, some companies have a policy of rejecting claims with the slightest complications," she explained. "Then some people will just forget about them or give up and accept the rejection. Most people would win if they would file an appeal, but many won't. A lot of older people tend to accept insurance rejections without question." Another problem she noticed is that complicated claims, particularly those that a novice or poorly trained adjuster might not understand, get shuffled into a "pending" file and can sit there for months. All the patient gets in the meantime is a notice that more information is needed before the claim can be processed. "It's often a lot easier to say no," she said. "I was once called on the carpet because I wasn't rejecting enough claims. I saw claims adjusters reject payment for procedures just because the adjusters didn't understand them. I sometimes asked them, 'If this was your mother, wouldn't you want her to have as many tests and procedures as necessary for a diagnosis?'" Dennis's recommendation: "Keep asking for another review of your claim. Don't hesitate to contact your state insurance commission for assistance. Don't take no for an answer."

In addition to keeping careful watch on your insurance company, you should be alert for mistakes in bills coming directly from your doctor. Doctors may try to charge you for the part of their bills not paid by an insurer, even though their contract with the insurer stipulates that they will "write off" this money and not bill patients for it. Your insurer's EOB should indicate how much your doctor was paid, how much he or she was forced to write off, and how much—if anything—you owe. Do not pay a doctor bill for the amount of the write-off. If in doubt, call your insurance company and ask if the doctor who is billing you is under contract with the insurer and exactly what you are required to pay.

RESOLVE DISPUTES BEFORE PAYING MEDICAL BILLS

Don't be too quick to pay medical bills; wait until all the insurance issues are resolved. If you pay a bill and then your insurance company pays it later, not only are the chances of a screwup increased, but you'll have to go through the hassle of getting a refund. If your provider demands payment, simply explain that you are waiting to see what your insurance company pays.

Two examples from my own experience dealing with medical bills and insurance companies show just how much you can save by holding off on paying bills that come directly to you.

The first involved an $89 bill I received from a laboratory for a test. According to the statement on the bill, my insurer, Blue Cross Blue Shield of Kansas, had denied payment because it was not my primary insurance. While I was covered under a secondary retiree policy, Blue Cross Blue Shield of Kansas *was* my primary carrier and had always paid my medical bills as such. When I called the company, a customer service representative told me that the bill was not paid because the lab had submitted it to my secondary carrier first. When I called the lab, I discovered that it didn't even have a record of my secondary carrier. I called back Blue Cross Blue Shield. This time, a different representative told me that the bill was denied because Blue Cross Blue Shield had already paid for the services through another lab, which should have in turn paid the lab that was billing me. I called this second lab and learned that its billing office had mistakenly overlooked making its payment to the other lab. It's still not clear why the lab that was billing me concluded that Blue Cross Blue Shield was not my primary carrier, but by making a few phone calls up front instead of paying the bill, I was able to save myself the headache of trying to get reimbursed later by the lab.

The second example involved billing blunders on a much larger scale. I had received treatment from a New Jersey hospital that wound up costing $4,000. Several times the hospital submitted the bill to my New York insurer via electronic filing, but the bill kept disappearing into the ether. I made repeated calls to the hospital's customer service representatives, and eventually their supervisors, to tell them that my insurance company, with whom the hospital had a contract, had not received the bill. The hospital insisted my insurer had received the bill via the Internet and, more absurdly, refused to call my insurer to try to settle the matter or submit a duplicate bill by mail. For every call, I logged the details, because I knew from my policy booklet that the clock was ticking. After several months of phone calls, I alerted the hospital that my insurer would not pay a bill if it were submitted more than 180 days, or six months, after the charges were incurred. The hospital representatives continued to insist they had filed the bill correctly and demanded that I pay the bill since my insurer refused. But instead of capitulating and seeking reimbursement later, I stuck to the policy's rules. My insurer also advised me not to pay the bill and, for its part, insisted the hospital file the bill correctly. Finally, after about a year, the hospital discovered that there was a glitch in its electronic filing system that had made the bill go awry. The hospital finally filed the paperwork—and my insurer promptly rejected it because it had been filed after the six-month cutoff date. My insurer also informed the hospital that under the terms of its contract I was not responsible for any payment toward the bill. I never heard from the hospital again. That was $4,000 saved and a good lesson in why you shouldn't be too quick to pay medical bills covered by insurance. Had I paid this bill, I could have had a difficult time persuading the hospital to give me a refund.

Sorting through and resolving these problems is complex, confusing, and time-consuming. If the amount involved is not large, many people simply pay rather than confront their insurers. That's a mistake. "Some people say, 'Who cares about fifty-seven dollars?' or some similar amount," said Susan A. Dressler, a claims assistance professional in Chicago who makes a living helping people deal with their insurers. "But that's how insurance companies make a lot of money. If you multiply these kinds of small figures by the hundreds of thousands of people some companies insure, it's a huge amount." Or simply consider how you could spend the $57 on something that really *isn't* covered by your insurance.

Since sloppiness and delays that result from it work to the benefit of insurance companies, a health-care log and organized files can go far in saving you money. Dressler said most insurance companies are notoriously bad at "handling paper." Simply, "they lose things," she said. "They say they never received documents that people have faxed or mailed to them several times." My experience certainly bears this out. Lost claims and paperwork became such a frequent problem with one insurer I had several years ago that I started sending everything by certified mail with a return receipt requested. For a few extra dollars, depending on the documents' weight, things suddenly stopped going missing.

A PRO ON YOUR SIDE

Our health-care system requires a vast amount of paperwork. If you have a serious illness, accident, or surgery, not only do you have to worry about your health and whether your insurance company will cover the bills, but you have to contend with the onslaught of occasionally incomprehensible bills and insurance EOBs. Cutting through the medical-billing bureaucracy can seem like a full-time job. As a letter to the editor of the *New York Times* summed it up: "By forcing patients to spend months fighting to recoup out-of-pocket costs or avoid paying unwarranted bills, insurers increase the chances that patients will simply give up, too occupied with the daily grind of work, family obligations and (most cynically) their illnesses to spend hours a week battling unfriendly 'customer service' personnel about unhelpful forms."

If you are overwhelmed by confusing bills and EOBs or don't feel up to the task of dealing with them, you could consider hiring a claims assistance professional, or CAP, like Susan Dressler, to do the work, including negotiating with your insurer, for you. But first, if you are covered by an employer-provided insurance plan, ask your company's human resources staff or benefits coordinator to help. Sometimes they will bird-dog claims for you, sometimes not.

Most CAPs charge by the hour. Dressler's hourly rate is $90, but CAPs in small towns and more rural areas are less expensive, sometimes charging as little as $30 an hour. A few charge a percentage of the money they recover from your insurer, but you should be cautious of this arrangement; after all, most, if not all, of the money a CAP recovers doesn't go to you but to your health-care providers, and, with medical bills so big, you could end up with a hefty tab due to your CAP. For that reason, most people are probably better off with a predictable hourly rate. Just get an up-front estimate of how many hours your claim might take. Dressler said a lot of simple problems can be handled in an hour or so; some complicated claims, especially those dealing with reasonable-and-customary-charge issues, can take up to twenty hours. Like many in her field, she does not charge for an initial consultation. "If I can't help somebody, I'm not going to charge them," she explained.

Dressler is sometimes able to push an insurer for a quick resolution to a problem. She recalled a disabled client who went on short-term disability and six months later had not received a single monthly check, despite placing calls and sending faxes to the insurance company. Soon after Dressler took over the case, the company started sending checks. "I can often get things resolved because I know what questions to ask and what information to provide," she said. "People are also sometimes a bit timid about calling their insurance company. They might not know how to file an appeal." It probably helps when an insurer hears that a client has hired someone to pursue a claim through every conceivable channel.

Among her tactics, Dressler urges patients to request a full copy of their hospital bill, which they normally would not receive. "If you look at your full hospital bill, I bet you'll find things on it you never had," she mentioned. "I once had an eighty-five-year-old lady call me about a hospital bill that included a 'cadaver kit,' even though she had been discharged from the hospital. 'Doesn't that mean I didn't make it?' she asked. 'It does,' I told her. The charge was removed from her bill."

Dressler is well suited for what she does. She started her company—Health Claim Assistance (www.healthclaimassistance .net)—in 1990 after working for nearly two decades in the insurance industry dealing with claims. In 1997, she started the Alliance of Claims Assistance Professionals (www.claims.org), which provides help to consumers as well as to those who wish to become claims assistance professionals. Through the Web site, you can find the names and contact information of CAPs in your state.

Like Nancy Dennis, Dressler is suspicious of some insurance industry practices. "I have a pretty good feeling that some insurance companies deny as many claims as possible on the theory that a certain percentage of people will just pay the bills themselves," she said.

8

Planning for Medicare

People like Medicare because it doesn't punish the sick.

—DIANE ARCHER, FOUNDER,
THE MEDICARE RIGHTS CENTER

The headlines and television news teasers that accompany the annual report on Medicare, usually issued each March, can be downright scary. Almost always they trumpet the word *bankruptcy* or *broke*, along with a date in the not-too-distant future when Medicare will default and seniors will be faced with financial disaster.

There's only one problem: The doomsday reports are not true. At the very least, such warnings are a "distortion and a disservice," according to Robert M. Hayes, president of the Medicare Rights Center, a nonprofit organization that helps people with Medicare problems. John L. Palmer, one of two appointed public trustees for Social Security and Medicare, calls it "wrong to say Medicare will go broke," adding that the situation "was not as dire as headlines would have you believe."

I guess it depends on your definition of *broke*. For instance, the Medicare trustees' report for 2005 stated that Medicare's hospital insurance trust fund is expected to exhaust its *surplus* by 2018. But the hospital fund, known as Medicare Part A, gets its money from the Medicare payroll tax, which would continue to be collected, so the fund will still be able to pay 80 percent of its bills. Part A accounts for around 50 percent of the Medicare program's spending. Medicare Part B, which pays for doctor bills and other outpatient services, gets 25 percent of its money from the premiums paid by beneficiaries and the remaining 75 percent from general tax revenues; it would not be affected at all by the depletion of the hospital fund's surplus.

What this boils down to: By 2018, Medicare may not be able to pay 20 percent of a 50 percent chunk of its bills unless it can find some extra money from somewhere. That represents an overall short-fall of about 10 percent for all Medicare spending combined. If this is the definition of *broke,* a lot of families, companies, and the government fall into that category.

Also, it is a thirteen-year projection. The problem is that eco-nomic guesswork does not always have a great track record. In a field like medicine, financial projections are especially difficult. "Medicare projections are based on anticipated increases in medical costs, which are very unreliable because of things like advances in technology," Hayes explained, pointing out that the percentage of Medicare spending for hospitals is shrinking because new medi-cines and technologies are allowing treatments outside of hospitals as well as shorter stays. Hayes added that "the whole focus of the new prescription drug program is to treat more people pharmaceu-tically so they may not need hospital care. Less high blood pressure and fewer heart attacks mean less hospitalization." Palmer, who is an economist and a professor at Syracuse University's Maxwell School of Citizenship and Public Affairs, agreed that "there is certainly a high degree of uncertainty attached to any long-term projection about medical costs."

Health-care prices are rising, but efforts to turn more of Medicare over to private health maintenance organizations and managed-care companies are also running up costs. Medicare's administrative expenses total about 2 percent of the full budget, whereas for private insurers the figure hits 12 to 18 percent, or even more, to cover expenses like advertising, executive salaries and bonuses, complex claims processing, and lobbying. "HMOs and managed-care companies can't compete with Medicare," Hayes said. "Their Medicare plans run about ten percent more than traditional fee-for-service Medicare. One reason for this is that because Medicare is so big, insurers can't match it on economies of scale."

Hayes contends that because of this cost difference, the political battle over Medicare has turned the liberal-conservative argument on its head: "You normally think of conservatives as being concerned about keeping federal spending down. They are saying we have to reduce Medicare outlays, but at the same time they are pushing these wildly expensive HMOs and PPOs. A significant piece of Medicare expense is the high costs of privatization. The conservatives, by pushing privatization, end up calling for spending more, not less, money. But if you say often enough that privatization saves money, people buy it."

A POLITICAL BATTLE

Medicare's budget projections get tremendous media attention because the program has grown into a big piece of the federal budget. It is under assault from two groups: deficit hawks and ideologically motivated politicians and policy experts who think the federal government should not be involved with any social programs, whether Medicare, Social Security, education, or welfare. But if you are age sixty or older and are counting on Medicare to pay your health bills, should you be worried about the calls to "reform" Medicare or Medicare's seemingly bleak numbers? No.

Just as it is unlikely that the projected 10 percent shortfall in 2018 will spell the end of Medicare, the advocates for killing the program are unlikely to taste much success. Despite the attacks, Medicare remains immensely popular with the approximately 43 million Americans covered by it, and little wonder. Its coverage is relatively comprehensive, and its beneficiaries do not have to cope with the complex bureaucracy of commercial insurance, with its myriad policies, exclusions, limitations, and fine print. Medicare is also popular with beneficiaries' children and grandchildren, who do not have to worry that medical bills will overwhelm subsequent generations, as was the fear before President Lyndon B. Johnson signed Medicare into law in 1965. Another plus for Medicare is choice. Some reform-minded politicians have argued that encouraging Medicare patients to enroll in private-plan Medicare HMOs and PPOs offers the elderly more "choices." Yet the choice most people want is to be able to choose their own doctors. Henry Aaron, the Brookings Institution authority on health-care financing, sees a "certain irony" here. "With private insurance, you have a choice of plans but not of doctors and hospitals," he said. "Traditional Medicare gives you no choice of plans but an unlimited choice of doctors and hospitals."

THE DETAILS YOU NEED TO KNOW ABOUT MEDICARE

Since Medicare is going to be around for a long time, you need to understand it and prepare for it. Medicare provides health insurance for:

- People sixty-five years old or older.
- People under age sixty-five who have been receiving Social Security Disability Insurance for more than two years.
- People under age sixty-five who have permanent kidney failure requiring continuing dialysis or a kidney transplant.
- People under age sixty-five who have been diagnosed with amyotrophic lateral sclerosis, commonly known as Lou Gehrig's disease.

Medicare consists of three main programs. **Part A**, as discussed earlier, covers hospital bills. You cannot opt out of Part A and are automatically enrolled in it when you turn sixty-five. There are no monthly premiums for the program; you "prepaid" for the coverage through the Medicare taxes deducted from your payroll checks.

Part B covers doctors' bills and outpatient services. You must choose to enroll in Part B; most people do. The Part B premium, which increases every year, was set at $88.50 per month for 2006 (a 13 percent increase from 2005). Note that if you are receiving Social Security benefits, increases in Medicare Part B effectively wipe out all or most of your annual Social Security cost-of-living raise.

Part D covers prescription drugs. A fuller discussion of Part D and other prescription drug options is included in chapter 6.

While Medicare covers a lot, it does not cover everything. If you are enrolled in the traditional fee-for-service Medicare program, which allows you to use virtually any doctor or hospital you choose, you almost certainly need a supplemental insurance policy, called a Medigap policy as discussed later in this chapter. (If you are under age sixty-five and covered by Medicare, you may not be able to buy this supplemental insurance until you turn sixty-five.) Just take a look at what, for 2006, traditional Medicare does not cover.

- A deductible of $952 for the first sixty days you are in the hospital.
- Coinsurance of $238 a day for hospitalization for days sixty-one through ninety and $476 a day for stays beyond day ninety of a benefit period.
- An annual deductible of $124 for Medicare Part B.
- A 20 percent coinsurance payment for physicians and most outpatient services through Part B.

If you are discharged from the hospital and have to go back after sixty days have passed, a new benefit period starts and you incur

Figure 10

Some Medicare Gaps, 2006

Part A: Hospitalization	You owe up to:
Deductible for first 60 days in the hospital	$ 952
A second stay of 60 days or less within a year, but in a new benefit period	1,904
A third stay of 60 days or less within a year, but in a new benefit period	2,856
Coinsurance for hospital days 61 through 90	$238 a day
Coinsurance for hospital days after the 90th	$476 a day
Doing the math:	
Hospital charges for a 90-day stay	*$ 8,092*
Hospital charges for a 120-day stay	*22,372*

Part B: Doctors and outpatient services	
Premium at $88.50 per month	$ 1,062
Deductible, annual	124
Coinsurance	20% of charges

the $952 deductible again. (If you return within sixty days of your discharge, you do not.) This deductible can become a big number—$1,904 or $2,856—if you have to be hospitalized two or three times a year and never go back into the hospital less than sixty days after your previous stay.

There are also charges of more than $100 a day for days twenty-one through one hundred in a skilled nursing facility, and charges for blood if you need a transfusion. And Medicare premiums, deductibles, copays, and coinsurance can all increase yearly. Two Web sites are helpful in explaining Medicare charges in detail. The first, www.medicare.gov, is run by the Centers for Medicare and Medicaid Services (toll free, 1-800-MEDICARE). The second, www.medicarerights.org, is operated by the nonprofit Medicare

Rights Center, which is based in New York City and, among other things, helps people with Medicare problems and questions.

THE MEDICARE ADVANTAGE PROGRAM

Because of the deductibles and gaps in Medicare coverage, most people purchase a Medigap policy or enroll in a private Medicare HMO or PPO plan in their area under the Medicare Advantage program, which pays private insurers for each Medicare recipient they insure. Both kinds of private HMO or PPO plans usually offer more coverage than traditional Medicare, sometimes including limited vision and dental benefits. Note that you cannot combine a Medigap policy with the Medicare Advantage program.

If you enroll in a private Medicare Advantage plan, you almost always have to pay an extra premium on top of the Medicare Part B premium to the insurer. There's also the option under Medicare Advantage of joining a Medicare PFFS, or private fee-for-service plan. A PFFS operates much like traditional Medicare, except that you must choose providers that accept the plan's payment terms. According to the federal Centers for Medicare and Medicaid Services, Medicare Advantage plans result in average beneficiary savings of $100 a month. However, under these private plans you are limited to certain doctors, hospitals, and—in the case of HMOs and PPOs—certain geographic service areas. In addition, as with all private insurance, there can be extra copayments or limitations if you have a serious illness. In a Medicare Advantage HMO or PPO, Part D, the voluntary drug coverage, may also be offered but will require an extra premium. The prices vary greatly, but the average premium for prescription coverage through Medicare Advantage is about $32 a month.

If you elect a Medicare Advantage HMO, PPO, or PFFS plan (all three are not available in every area of the country), your extra monthly premium buys you coverage for many of the charges you would be responsible for paying out of pocket under traditional

Medicare if you do not have a Medigap policy. The choice between a Medigap policy and Medicare Advantage comes down to how comfortable you are with managed care and using only doctors or hospitals in a certain network. (Only about 12 percent of Medicare recipients are enrolled in Medicare Advantage plans.) Premiums vary widely across the country. For 2005, Humana's premiums for a Medicare HMO were as much as $50 a month; for a PPO, up to $119; and for a PFFS, as much as $139—all depending on location. In New York City, Empire Blue Cross Blue Shield of New York sells a Medicare HMO without Part D prescription coverage for $83 a month; for a PPO, $150 a month. Prices are always quoted per person; family coverage is not available. Medicare Advantage rates are community rated, meaning they are the same regardless of your health status or age.

Keep in mind that if you continue to work after age sixty-five and have employer-sponsored coverage, Medicare becomes your secondary insurance until you quit working. If you have retiree health benefits, your employer-sponsored insurance can be used as your Medigap policy when you retire. A warning: If you're still working at age sixty-five and have employer-sponsored coverage but no retiree benefits, be very careful about signing up for Medicare Part B. That's because if you try to purchase a Medigap policy more than six months after signing up for Medicare Part B, an insurance company can deny you coverage because of preexisting conditions or charge you more. During the first six months' window after you start Plan B, however, an insurer may not deny you any Medigap policy it sells, may not make you wait for coverage to start, and may not charge you more for a policy because of preexisting health problems. When you receive the paperwork for Medicare Part A, you must check a box if you *do not* want Part B at that time. If you do not check the box, you start the six-month clock ticking.

Diane Archer, the founder of the Medicare Rights Center who is a special counsel to the group and serves on its board, recommends passing up Medicare Advantage and choosing traditional Medicare plus a Medigap policy—that is, if you can afford it. While Medicare Advantage offers lower premiums for now, copays and coinsurance are increasing for these plans. The private plans also cost taxpayers more than Medicare, so Congress is likely to slash spending on them, thus reducing benefits or increasing costs, before any other part of the program. If you get a serious illness, Medicare Advantage also has gaps of its own: There can be restrictions on access to some treatments.

Geography can also be a bigger issue than you might expect. Archer cited problems with continuity of care and service-area limits. Doctors and other providers are allowed to drop in and out of the plans, and the plans themselves can pull out of your area at any time—leaving you scrambling to find new coverage. If you travel a lot, you probably do not want to be restricted to a Medicare Advantage plan's service area. This can also cause troubles if you become ill and temporarily need to live with a relative outside your service area.

"Older and disabled people often sign up for these Medicare HMOs and other Medicare Advantage plans to save money, which they will—as long as they're relatively healthy and stay in-network," Archer said. "But if they get a serious illness, they may find that certain copays are astronomical. People like Medicare because it doesn't punish the sick. If you have traditional Medicare and good supplemental coverage, which most people do, there are no out-of-pocket costs. You've budgeted for your health care for the year. Everybody is paying the same amount of money, no matter what services or care they require. That's what insurance is supposed to be."

It is important to remember that if you sign up for a Medicare Advantage plan, you forgo a Medigap policy. Moreover, if you change your mind a year or so later, you might have trouble getting a Medigap policy because the six-month window for getting a guaranteed-issue policy will have expired. If your Medicare Advantage plan dumps your coverage by pulling out of your geographic area, this restriction will not be applied to you. In addition, if you live in one of the five states with guaranteed-issue laws on the books—Maine, Massachusetts, New Jersey, New York, and Vermont—the restriction will not pose a problem since you are guaranteed coverage no matter what. Even with guaranteed-issue laws, though, there can be waiting periods before preexisting conditions are covered, and by choosing a Medicare Advantage plan you could expose yourself to significant charges during the waiting period if you decide to switch down the road.

OVERVIEW OF MEDIGAP POLICIES

As it happens, the government has made it fairly easy to buy Medigap insurance. You get to choose from among twelve standardized policies, A through L. (Massachusetts, Minnesota, and Wisconsin have different standardized plans.) This standardization, according to Robert Hayes of the Medicare Rights Center, has led to a "reasonably good level of customer satisfaction with Medigap policies." Generally, the higher the letter the better the coverage, though this rule does not apply to G, K, and L. Plan G does not cover the $124 annual deductible for Medicare Part B and pays only 80 percent of any excess charges not covered by Part B, as compared to other Medigap plans that offer the benefit at 100 percent. Plans K and L are relatively new, low-cost alternatives to Plans A through J but have fewer benefits. Instead of receiving 100 percent coverage, you receive 50 percent (Plan K) or 75 percent (Plan L) for some of the most common Part B charges. The annual maximum out-of-pocket limit on your payments is $4,000 for Plan K and $2,000 for Plan L. The prices for these low-cost Medigap policies may seem attractive, but you could end up spending a lot if you have a serious illness.

Insurance companies don't have to offer every Medigap plan, but the ones they do offer must have the same levels of coverage as those offered by other insurers. When you're shopping for insurance, the main difference you need to look for is price, which is not regulated.

Medigap plans H, I, and J—which offer limited prescription drug coverage—are no longer available for new enrollment because of the Medicare Part D prescription drug plan. Those already enrolled in one of these plans when Part D was rolled out on January 1, 2006, were allowed to keep their coverage, but many wisely switched to another Medigap plan prior to the May 2006 deadline for initial enrollment. That's because if you have Plan H, I, or J and decide now to switch to Part D, which has better drug coverage, you face a post-deadline penalty. According to Deane Beebe of the Medicare Rights Center, premiums for H, I, and J are likely to increase over time as those enrolled in the plans get older and have expenses for medical bills that are not balanced by premiums coming in from new Medicare recipients.

Figure 11 shows the benefits of the various Medigap plans. Note that the least expensive, but also least comprehensive, Plan A, does not cover the $952 deductible for your first sixty days of hospitalization. Remember, too, that you could be hit with this deductible two or three times in a single calendar year. If you are on a limited income, consider paying a little extra for Plan B instead. The most popular plans, C and F, are among the most comprehensive.

PAYING FOR THE GAP

Medigap policies can be priced three ways:

Attained age means your premium will increase as you get older. Most attained-age policies set an age after which no more age-related increases kick in.

Issue age means your premium is based on your age when you bought the policy and won't increase because you get older.

Figure 11

Medigap Plans, 2006

— Plans —

Gaps in Medicare Part A

	A	B	C	D	E	F	G	K	L
Hospital deductible *Covers $952 in each benefit period*		●	●	●	●	●	●	50%*	75%*
Hospital coinsurance *Days 61–90 ($238) and days 91–150 ($476) in hospital*	●	●	●	●	●	●	●	●	●
First three pints of blood	●	●	●	●	●	●	●	50%*	75%*
Hospital care coinsurance	●	●	●	●	●	●	●	50%*	75%*
Emergency care outside the United States *80% of costs during the first 60 days of each trip, after an annual deductible of $250, up to a maximum benefit of $1,600 per year*			●	●	●	●	●		

Gaps in Medicare Part B

	A	B	C	D	E	F	G	K	L
Annual deductible *Covers $124*			●			●			
Services coinsurance *Includes doctors' services, laboratory and X-ray services, durable medical equipment, and hospital outpatient services*	●	●	●	●	●	●	●	50%*	75%*

— continued —

Figure 11

Medigap Plans, 2006 *continued*

Gaps in Medicare Part B

	— Plans —								
	A	B	C	D	E	F	G	K	L
Excess charges benefits *Under federal law, the excess limit is 15% more than Medicare's approved charge when the provider does not accept Medicare assignment (under New York law, it is 5% for most services)*						100%	80%		
Preventive medical care *Up to $120 per year for non-Medicare-covered physicals, preventive tests, and services*					●				
Preventive medical care *100% of coinsurance for Part B–covered preventive care services, after the Part B deductible has been paid*	●	●	●	●	●	●	●	●	●
Skilled nursing facility daily coinsurance *Covers $119 per day for days 21–100 in each benefit period, up to 3 periods per year*			●	●	●	●	●	50%*	75%*
At-home recovery benefit *Covers $119 per day for days 21–100 in each benefit period, up to 3 periods per year*				●			●		

*Out of pocket maximums
Pays 100% of Part A and Part B coinsurance after annual maximum has been spent

Plan K: $4,000   **Plan L:** $2,000

Source: Medicare Rights Center

Community rated means everyone pays the same premium regardless of age.

No matter how your policy is priced, premiums will rise with inflation in the cost of medical services; you, however, cannot be singled out for a rate increase based on your medical condition.

Let's look at a sampling of some Medigap prices around the country. Since Plan F offers comprehensive coverage and is the most popular, we'll compare rates for policies under that plan. (As with many of the prices quoted in this book, they may have changed by the time of publication.)

Blue Cross Blue Shield of Kansas, which uses attained-age pricing for its Medigap policies, offers Plan F at $101.46 a month, or $1,217.52 a year, at age sixty-five. The premium increases each year as you grow older to $177.13 a month, or $2,125.56 a year, at age eighty. Past age eighty, there are no more age-related increases. Remember, however, that there can be other across-the-board rate increases linked to inflation.

Blue Cross Blue Shield of Tennessee, which also uses attained-age pricing for its Medigap policies, has rates for Plan F that run from $92.14 a month, or $1,105.68 a year, at age sixty-five, to $216.30 a month, or $2,595.60 a year, at age ninety-one.

In Idaho, Regence Blue Shield uses a combination of issue-age and attained-age pricing that is weighted toward issue age. If you are between ages sixty-five and sixty-nine, Plan F will cost $159 a month, or $1,908 a year; for those seventy to seventy-four, it's $185 a month, or $2,220 a year; between seventy-five and seventy-nine, $191 a month, or $2,292 annually; age eighty or older, $207 a month, or $2,484 a year. Your rates will change as you enter each category, but not as much as for attained-age pricing: The difference between the Idaho premiums at age sixty-five and at age seventy-four is $26 a month; in Kansas, that difference would be $37.44; and in Tennessee, it would be $54.85. So while the Idaho plan might be more expensive to start, the difference drops as you grow older.

New York is a community-rated state, so the prices for Medigap policies are the same for everyone, regardless of age or health, although the state is divided into two areas for pricing. Empire Blue Cross Blue Shield's "downstate" (read: New York City metropolitan area) price is $199.72 a month, or $2,396.64 a year. For the rest of the state, it's $179.24 a month, or $2,150.88 annually.

As you can see from these examples, a policy that is priced by attained age does start out cheaper at first, but the price will rise more over time than an issue-age policy. You simply have to look at the policies and pricing available in your area and get out your calculator to decide which works best for you. In many cases, the cheapest issue-age or community-rated policy may be best in the long run. Keep in mind that no matter what a Medigap policy's price is, *the benefits are exactly the same from all companies offering that policy.* The only difference is price, which can vary widely among policies offered by different companies in the same state or region. According to a retirement planning guide published by Kiplinger's, Plan F prices for a sixty-five-year-old man in West Palm Beach, Florida, ranged from $2,172 to $3,165 a year; in Chicago, the range was $1,305 to $2,954.

If you are in the market for a Medigap policy, here are some important points to remember:

- While you should shop for the best price, since policy benefits in each category are exactly the same, you should also consider the rating of an insurance company. Look for insurers whose financial strength is listed at B+ or better by the insurance-rating agency A. M. Best Company (www.ambest.com). This "very good" or better rating is an indication of how well a company can meet its ongoing obligations to policyholders. It may also be an indication of the speed and quality of service.

- You have six months from the time you enroll in Medicare Part B to be able to buy a Medigap policy with no wait for coverage to start (if you had previous coverage) and without preexisting conditions being an issue. The policy must be guaranteed renewable. If you wait longer than six months, though, you could be turned down or charged more. Some exceptions are if your Medicare Advantage plan drops you, your retiree health plan is canceled, or your Medigap insurance company goes bankrupt. The Medicare Web site (www.medicare.gov) has a complete list of exceptions and details about them, along with various publications and guides that you can print out.
- All prices for Medigap policies are per person, although there may be some discounts for females, nonsmokers, and/or married people.
- Generally, you can switch Medigap policies only by selecting a new one with *fewer* benefits.
- Medicare generally does not cover you outside the country. If you travel overseas, make sure your Medigap policy will pay for emergency care outside the United States.
- Don't hesitate to ask for help or advice if you don't understand something. No book or Web site can explain everything. You can call Medicare directly at 1-800-MEDICARE. Each state also maintains offices and departments that can help. The Kaiser Family Foundation Web site (www.kff.org) is a good source for contact information for individual states.

MEDICARE FOR ALL?

Diane Archer, the founder of the Medicare Rights Center, is campaigning to bring Medicare to all, not just those who are sixty-five. Although she concedes it's an uphill battle, she is convinced it is the best way to make sure everyone has medical coverage.

"It would not only be the simplest and cheapest way, but also a really good way to make sure that all Americans have coverage," she said. "Some projections show that it would cost less than what we now spend on health care. Medicare is just a much more effective and cost-efficient way of delivering health care and guaranteeing that everyone gets coverage. It is the perfect public-private partnership: government funding and private health-care providers." An e-mail message from a *New York Times* reader to the columnist Paul Krugman explained very succinctly why Medicare-for-all might save money: "I realize that its present per-patient cost is high because of the age of those who qualify for Medicare, but if the pool were enlarged by including most all Americans, wouldn't the per-patient cost decrease? By eliminating the profits built into private health insurance companies, we could save even more money. Plus, when ill, many uninsured people presently use a hospital emergency room because they do not have medical insurance, but if they were covered by a national health insurance, they could be treated in a doctor's office, which is less costly than a hospital."

Archer argues that the problem with private health insurance plans is that they "just give you a choice of how you want to limit your coverage, whether limited to doctors or hospitals or to certain illnesses or diseases." She called such restrictions, especially on treatments like chemotherapy, "shocking," adding that "the whole push toward consumer-directed health care is a push toward having more people underinsured." As she put it: "Right now we're on a Darwinian trajectory: survival of the fittest. We'll continue on that trajectory until leaders start galvanizing the public around a solution."

Medicare is popular, according to Archer, because it works. "It's more efficient than any other system," she said. "When you talk to people on the ground, they all love Medicare because it's fair and gives them access to the care they need, when they need it, at a price they can afford."

9

The Threat to Your Savings and Retirement

What was awful to me was that I would have to find a new doctor.
All my connections with health services would be gone.

—RICHARD BEACH, ON SWITCHING RETIREE HEALTH PLANS

As we have seen, more medical costs are being pushed onto consumers, often accompanied with clever catchphrases like "more choice" and "ownership society." But, in fact, the changes under way in the American health-care system are more likely to limit your choices and leave you the owner of an increasingly large pile of medical bills. The result: a steady whittling away of your savings and retirement income—not to mention your peace of mind. James Surowiecki, in one of his financial columns in the *New Yorker*, pointed out that what is really afoot with medical costs, as well as with disappearing pensions, is a massive shifting of risk from the corporation to the individual. The problem, Surowiecki wrote, is that "workers are not being compensated with higher wages for taking on all this new risk." In fact, he noted that real wages have actually fallen since 2001 and the average household income is only slightly above what it was in 1973.

Increased worker health-care costs—in the form of higher pre-miums, copayments, and coinsurance—without a corresponding increase in pay means you have less money to spend and to save. The government and Wall Street are telling workers that they need to save more for retirement; at the same time, workers' ability to do so is constantly being eroded as companies shift more health costs to employees. At the beginning of 2006, Sears forced its re-tirees to begin paying the full cost of their retiree coverage, an in-crease of several hundred dollars a month for most, as well as reducing medical benefits for current workers. A month later, Nis-san, the Japanese automaker, announced it was cutting health ben-efits for U.S. workers. Earlier, General Motors increased premiums and deductibles for workers and retirees. Moves like these are tak-ing place not just at troubled retailers and automobile manufactur-ers or bankrupt airlines. Many companies, including very profitable ones, are using such money-saving tactics. The Com-merce Department reported in January 2006 that Americans' per-sonal savings rate for 2005 dropped into negative territory for the first time since the Great Depression. The rate fell to minus 0.5 percent, meaning that Americans spent all their after-tax income that year plus had to dip into savings or increase borrowing. The media's reports on America's negative savings rate cited increased spending for big-ticket items like cars and the psychological effect of the housing boom, which has made many consumers feel wealthier. But what about extra money workers have to pay for their health-related expenses? Savings are being eaten away by the spiraling costs of health care.

In addition to higher premiums, copays, and coinsurance, work-ers and retirees face disruptions in the continuity of their health care as employers routinely switch coverage plans in favor of less expensive ones in efforts to control costs. The new health plans may or may not cover the doctors and health-care providers workers have been using. Being forced to find new providers—and getting health-care records transferred—is more than a hassle; it can genuinely affect quality of care.

ONE MAN'S TOUGH CHOICES

Richard Beach retired from the Indianapolis public school system in 2002 at age fifty-nine after teaching elementary music for twenty-eight years. He was luckier than many retirees: The system allowed him to keep his single-person medical coverage—but he had to pay for it. As part of his retirement package, he did, however, receive $10,000 to help offset the monthly premiums of about $500 for his HMO. If you do the math, you know that the $10,000 ran out after less than two years. "Several years ago that ten thousand dollars might have paid for my premiums until I was sixty-five and eligible for Medicare," he said. "But no more. The ten thousand has stayed the same while insurance premiums have zoomed up."

But in 2004 he got a break. By accepting higher copayments for doctor visits under a new program offered by his HMO, he was able to reduce his premiums to $300 a month. He was in a pretty sweet spot. His premiums had gone down by $200 a month—an effective increase in his retirement income—and he was able to maintain the same network of doctors and health-care providers that he had been using for more than twenty years.

That sweet spot turned sour the next year. In the fall of 2005, Beach was notified that his premiums would jump to $847 a month—an increase of $547—beginning in January 2006. His only option was to switch to a less expensive, and presumably less comprehensive, HMO that was also offered by the system. It would cost $387 a month—$87 more than he had been paying, but $460 a month less than keeping his old plan. That option, however, would mean giving up his longtime doctors and health providers. And, in either case, his retirement income would be reduced. "There was never any official reason given for this," he said. "But clearly medical costs had increased.

It's tempting to blame the school system, but the school system didn't raise the rates. The health-care industry raised the rates."

At first Beach felt his only option was to pay the higher premium in order to maintain continuity in his health care. "I was very stressed," he said. "What was awful to me was that I would have to find a new doctor. All my connections with health services would be gone. The system gave us a big book of providers for the cheaper system, but I didn't know any of them."

Finally, a friend recommended a physician near Beach's home who was part of the new HMO. He visited the new doctor's office and was satisfied that it would be acceptable. So he switched to the new HMO, partly because of the money and partly because of his friend's recommendation. He said that after transferring his medical records to the new doctor, things went smoothly and he has been "more or less" satisfied with the new plan. Despite the stress and disruption in care, he knows he is fortunate to be among the insured.

BALANCING COSTS AND COVERAGE

As the U.S. health-care crisis plays out, many people are going to be whipsawed by high prices and diminished coverage—both of which threaten their nest eggs. While individuals are limited in what they can do to mitigate the problem, there are some steps that can help.

- **If you have a menu of coverage options, pick the one that strikes a balance between saving you money and providing the kind of health care you want.** Reconsider any qualms you might have about the restrictions of an HMO. An HMO is probably the cheapest and most comprehensive coverage available to you. It also requires less paperwork and record keeping, and most HMOs have improved since the 1980s and 1990s, when horror stories abounded. Sure, a PPO or an indemnity plan will give you more choices—but at a higher price that may eat up more of your savings.

- If you are healthy and can afford to fund a linked savings account, opt for a health savings account. With their tax breaks and cheaper premiums, HSAs can save you money. Of course, you may want to reassess your choice if you find yourself spending down all your account's tax-free money to pay deductibles. But as the examples in chapter 4 showed, you could spend a big chunk of that money and still be ahead of the game.

- Take advantage of a flexible spending account, or FSA, if your employer offers one. It allows you to use tax-free earnings, usually up to $5,000, to pay for medical bills not covered by insurance. But because you must spend the money set aside in your FSA in a given year or lose it, set up an FSA budget so that you know exactly what you will spend.

- If your health-care expenses are rising and you cannot find cheaper coverage, look at ways to cut back on spending elsewhere so you can at least maintain some level of savings as you pay higher health-care bills. In *Live Well on Less Than You Think: The New York Times Guide to Achieving Your Financial Freedom*, I make the case that we live in such a rich society that the average person can cut spending significantly without onerous sacrifices. The money can add up to thousands of dollars a year, enough to cover many people's increased health costs.

- Remain as flexible as possible. If you are forced to change doctors or your doctor leaves your insurance network, canvass your coworkers, friends, and even your current doctor about the providers who are in your new insurance network. It may even turn out you find someone you like better. Just be careful that all of your medical records get transferred properly, since fighting rejected claims will be more difficult if paperwork is missing. Keeping yourself covered is the important thing (and, of course, it will be better for your health).

WHAT ABOUT LONG-TERM-CARE INSURANCE?

One of the questions I am frequently asked, especially by older people, is whether they should purchase long-term-care insurance. I wish there was an easy answer.

There are several problems with long-term-care insurance. Deena Katz, the financial planner in Coral Gables, Florida, advocates such insurance in certain circumstances but points out that it hasn't been around that long. "Insurance companies have been in and out of these policies," she explained. "At one time there were one hundred fifty companies offering them; now there are very few. So the commitment is a little wobbly."

In addition, long-term-care insurance is getting more expensive and covering less; worse still, the regulations governing it are inconsistent. Existing policyholders can face premium increases, especially for policies that were underpriced as insurers tried to gain market share in recent years. The AARP Web site (www.aarp.org) cites the case of an Ohio couple who saw the annual premiums on their eight-year-old policy jump to $4,862 from $3,255, a 50 percent increase. While twenty-eight states have adopted model regulations to stablize premiums for long-term care based on recommendations by the National Association of Insurance Commissioners (NAIC), policies purchased before the regulations were passed in each state are not covered. If you already own long-term-care insurance, check to see if your policy is safe from indiscriminate premium increases. The NAIC Web site (www.naic.org) contains links to the various state insurance departments. Some of these links are helpful, some less so. In the end, you may have to contact your state insurance department for its regulations on long-term-care insurance.

The state-by-state reforms have made a difference in the value of long-term-care policies. Foremost, there is relatively better standardization of the policies than in the past. This is especially important, Katz noted, when it comes to the definitions of conditions and health events that will trigger benefit payments. Keep in mind, though, that long-term care is not age-specific: You don't have to be old and in a nursing home for it to start paying. Mary Lou Odle, a Kansas State University extension agent in Salina, Kansas, often helps people who are trying to understand long-term-care insurance. "Long-term policies vary," she said. "In addition to nursing-home care, they may cover home health care, assisted living, and adult day care."

According to Katz: "Long-term-care insurance is hard to understand, it varies with every state, and it is not the panacea we would like it to be. On the other hand, there are good uses for it. The reasons people should buy long-term care are for asset protection, estate preservation, and what I call the fear factor. If someone lives far away from family members and there is no one to take care of them, it is certainly a lot easier to go into a long-term-care facility as a paying patient than to have to go broke and accept Medicaid. The insurance is expensive, but you may be willing to accept a lesser quality of life today—in other words, bear the cost of buying the insurance—for the promise of tomorrow. The younger you are when you buy long-term-care insurance, of course, the less the premiums are."

Most experts agree that the two groups of people who should not purchase long-term-care insurance are those with high assets—enough money to afford care on their own—and those with low assets—too little money to worry about protecting it. The latter group should just count on Medicaid taking over after they have exhausted their resources. (The only problem: In many states, relying on Medicaid can adversely affect the assets of the spouse who doesn't need long-term care. You should seek advice on this topic from your county or state agency for the aging or elderly.)

The real conundrum, of course, is figuring out how high or low your assets must be to opt out of long-term care. Katz set $200,000 as the asset level, including equity in your home, below which you probably can't afford long-term-care insurance. But, she conceded, "there are disagreements about this all the time," and "some advisers say one hundred thousand dollars." Those with higher levels of assets just have to make decisions based on their cash flow and what they feel they can afford. Katz offered some sample costs: "The average nursing-home stay runs close to four thousand dollars a month. The average stay is about ninety days." That's $12,000. But further, Katz said, "Those that stay longer than that stay about three years. At the tail end of those statistics are people who are in nursing homes for many years."

What about those whose assets fall in the middle range? If you are single, aren't concerned about leaving an estate, or do not live far away from people who can help you, you may not need long-term-care insurance. Katz recommends that you also review your family medical background when making a decision. For instance, if a long-term, incapacitating illness, such as Alzheimer's disease or rheumatoid arthritis, runs in your family, the prospect of being responsible for years of residence in a nursing home might push you to buy a long-term-care policy.

You need to decide how long you can pay for long-term care on your own, Katz advised, adding that long-term-care insurance should be viewed as strictly catastrophic coverage. "If you can afford a short stay in a nursing home for a broken hip, you don't need the insurance for that," she said. "You want it for a five-year stay because you have Alzheimer's."

Katz warned that many people don't investigate the odds and the averages and don't really know how to buy long-term-care insurance. "Too many people are 'sold' this insurance," she contended. She urges her clients to buy only as much insurance as they need. "You may not need insurance to cover all your costs, or you may not be able to afford full coverage," she said. "Whatever you can afford to buy is going to defray some of the expense. If a nursing home is charging one hundred fifty dollars a day and you have a sixty-dollar-a-day policy, that's sixty dollars a day you don't have to spend." Katz also cautions against the pitch from many insurance companies that you need lifetime coverage. Katz says you really only need four to five years of coverage. Although it may be difficult to contemplate, the three-year average for longer nursing-home stays reflects the average life expectancy for people with serious, long-term illnesses.

Not surprisingly, Katz recommends consulting with a financial planner about long-term-care insurance. "Health care is getting harder," she said, "and we are living longer and longer." Some states offer tax incentives for buying long-term-care insurance. Don't forget to check with your employer's benefits department. Long-term care is sometimes offered through employers at much more favorable rates.

Even if you decide that long-term-care insurance is for you, you can be turned down for health reasons if you have preexisting medical conditions. "This is a big issue," Katz said, "and another reason than price for getting these policies earlier. You're less likely to have health problems at fifty than at seventy."

If a company turns you down for long-term-care insurance, don't despair. Try another. That's the lesson Mary H. "Jody" Parsons of Manhattan, Kansas, learned when she set out to buy the insurance after her husband died in March 2005, when she was seventy-three. One company, which required a physical exam, turned her down twice because of a relatively minor case of osteoarthritis in her right knee. But she applied to another company and was accepted simply on the basis of her medical records and a telephone interview. She bought a policy that will pay $70 a day for up to two years, or a bit over $51,000. Her premium is $111.16 a month, or $1,333.92 a year.

"Who knows if I'll need this or not?" Parsons said. "It's a crapshoot, but I think it's worth the gamble. I mainly wanted to protect my estate. I don't want to have to spend all my money on health care. I thought about buying life insurance instead, but that would have been too expensive."

10

Sorting Out Your Options

I got a crap job! Yeah, I make over minimum wage, but I got no benefits. The doctor says I got to have an operation. What the hell am I supposed to do?

—A NEW JERSEY SERVICE STATION ATTENDANT

The biggest problem with the American health-care system is that so many people—between 45.8 million and 81.8 million, depending on how they are counted—fall through the cracks. The feeble efforts coming out of Washington, D.C., to deal with this disgrace mainly involve expanding consumer-directed initiatives like health savings accounts. HSAs can be less expensive and may allow marginally more people to afford insurance policies, but they do nothing to address the issue of people who are uninsurable because of preexisting conditions. In the end, they may make things worse by peeling off the healthy and the wealthy, leaving everyone else behind with more expensive coverage. Some states are moving to close the coverage gap, but these efforts are at best a patchwork solution to a growing national problem.

The harsh truth is that for the next decade or so, you're on your own when it comes to our health coverage. Employer-based insurance is unraveling as more and more of its costs are being pushed onto workers. Buying individual insurance is becoming increasingly difficult and costly as insurers reposition themselves to contain their own financial risks.

Since you're on your own, you have to try to work the system to your advantage. The most important thing to remember as you search for the most coverage at the least cost is to remain flexible and resilient. Everything about health insurance is changing—usually not for the better—and your goal should be to limit the damage.

EMPLOYER-BASED COVERAGE

Clearly, the best and least expensive route to coverage for most people is through a job, although not all employers offer the benefit. If you are young and healthy, and your portion or your family's portion of employer-coverage premiums is hefty—say 50 to 100 percent— you may do better buying an individual health savings account (HSA), as described in chapter 4. This is partly because the group insurance through your job likely offers some coverage you may not need at all stages of your life—such as maternity benefits—or ever—such as mental health benefits. Later, of course, as your health needs change, you might want more comprehensive coverage. As discussed in chapter 5, individual coverage may be cheaper than employer coverage in most states because insurance companies are allowed to cherry-pick healthy customers; an employer must offer coverage to all workers, regardless of their health. If you decide to go the individual policy route and forgo employer coverage, proceed with care. Make sure you have the former policy signed and in hand before you reject the latter. You should never be without coverage. Even a few days without insurance can spell financial disaster if you suffer the onset of a serious illness or are badly injured in an accident. It can also make applying for individual insurance much more difficult.

Many employers offer a menu of plans for you to choose from, including an HMO, a PPO, and a traditional indemnity plan. Increasingly, HSAs are joining this lineup, and indemnity plans, the most expensive kind, are falling out of favor. During the so-called open-enrollment period each year, you can switch plans, and as you get older and health issues surface, you should actively consider this option every year. A young, healthy person should select an HMO—or an HSA if it's offered—to save on premium costs since he or she is less likely to use medical services than an older worker, who should investigate the benefit-premium trade-offs of signing up for a PPO or an indemnity plan that offers a wider variety of doctors and other providers.

An HSA might seem like a better low-premium option than an HMO, but despite having fewer service limitations, its high deductible makes it less useful for someone with a chronic medical problem. That's because you could run through the entire deductible each year and never build up pretax funds for future medical expenses in the HSA's linked savings account. In fact, the worst-case scenario for an HSA is that your expenses equal your deductible: You deplete your savings each year but never take advantage of the policy's coverage past the deductible.

The money you can save by switching your employer plan during open enrollment is not insignificant. For example, the difference in premiums between a PPO and an HMO can be quite large. If you find that your employer's HMO covers most of your doctors and providers and you can live with its restrictions, switching could be a good way to protect yourself from rising costs. A professor I know at Kansas State University recently switched to an HMO for that very reason. She had previously been covered under a PPO, whose premiums for a single person were $37.13 every other week; her new HMO premiums are $8.59, a savings of more than $700 a year. In addition, her out-of-pocket expenses, such as copayments, dropped. The trade-off for the savings: the usual restrictions of an

HMO. After some homework, however, she discovered that most of her existing doctors accepted the HMO, as did most other health-care providers where she lives.

There are some other ways either to increase your coverage or to save money with employer-sponsored insurance, especially if both you and your spouse work for employers that provide health benefits. You just have to do the calculation for your individual situation and goals. Consider the following:

- Get secondary coverage if possible. If both you and your spouse work and both have group health insurance available through your jobs, each can sign up for the insurance and list the other as a dependent. You won't receive double payments for medical bills, but coordinated benefits under the two plans will almost always pay 100 percent of the bills. This strategy usually works only with employer-based group insurance, not with individual policies; it may cost you more each month in premiums but can really pay off in the event of a serious illness or accident. Of course, if your portion of the premium on one or both policies is high, you need to weigh the extra expense against potential benefits.
- If your spouse works and has access to better or less expensive employer coverage than you, skip yours and sign yourself and your children up with your spouse's insurance as dependents. Your employer may even reward you with cash for declining coverage, provided you can show you have credible coverage elsewhere.
- Stay with your policy but let your spouse and children be covered by your spouse's employer coverage.
- If your employer pays most of your coverage premium cost but charges a lot, maybe even 100 percent, for coverage for your spouse and your children, keep your employer coverage but buy a less expensive individual policy for the rest of your family. This strategy will work only if your spouse and your children are healthy and have no preexisting conditions.

• Create a detailed Flexible Spending Account (FSA) budget, if your employer offers the program, to maximize your tax savings without losing money—through either unnecessary purchases or unused account balances.

INDIVIDUAL COVERAGE

As discussed in chapter 5, buying individual coverage is riskier than accepting employer coverage. For one thing, there is no open-enrollment period. What you are initially able to buy may be what you are stuck with, especially if you develop health problems. You generally can't be dumped or get stuck with a private rate increase if you become sick, but you could have trouble buying another policy.

While it's sometimes the case that the premium costs of an individual policy can be less than the overall cost of an employer-sponsored plan, many employers pick up the tab for much or most of the cost for their employees—so the cost to you is less. Concentrate on your bottom line: turn to an individual policy only if it saves *you* money. The good news is that individual policies can be quite inexpensive if you live in one of the forty-five states that do not guarantee their residents can purchase health insurance. The catch is you may not be able to buy coverage if you have a preexisting medical condition.

So what do you do if you have a preexisting condition?

Five states—Maine, Massachusetts, New Jersey, New York, and Vermont—have guaranteed-issue laws that protect people from being rejected by insurers for health reasons. Recently, the White House and Congress have pushed for more consumer-directed initiatives in the style of health savings accounts. But most of these proposals overlook the issue of preexisting conditions. In fact, associated health plans—one of the new bills that has passed the House and, although initially defeated, remains under consideration by the Senate, along with another measure in the House called the Health

Care Choice Act—could exacerbate the problems of preexisting conditions by effectively eliminating the power of state insurance commissions to regulate health care. If these bills become law, insurance companies operating in one state could sell health-care policies to groups of employees and individuals in another state even if the policies did not meet the standards of the second state—triggering a costly adverse selection effect that would spike the already steep price of insurance in the guaranteed-issue states.

If you have a preexisting condition, keep in mind that you might qualify for a federal or state assistance program such as Medicaid, even if you are employed. Though Medicaid may not be your best first option since so many doctors are refusing to accept it, any coverage is better than no coverage.

PRESCRIPTION DRUGS

If you have no prescription coverage, there are actually several options—as we saw in chapter 6—that can help you over this hurdle so you can buy the drugs you need. The three most important things you can do to lower prescription costs:

- Shop around for generic drugs. Wholesale prices are low, markups can be enormous, and retail prices are all over the place. There are specific retailers listed in chapter 6 that offer the cheapest generics.
- Buy brand-name drugs from Canada, where you can often save as much as 40 percent or more. Generics are cheaper, however, in the United States.
- Ask your doctor to prescribe a drug at double your needed dose and then split it. This will likely cut your cost in half, since the prices of drugs vary little with dosage strength. You'll save even more if you fill the prescription through a Canadian pharmacy. Pill-splitting doesn't work with all drugs, so check with your doctor first.

HELP FOR MANY

In the introduction, I pointed out that because of the nature of our health-care system, we are often forced to pick the best of several not-so-great options. In addition, until health care in America undergoes serious reform, current problems and the number of uninsured are likely to increase. What I have attempted to do in this book is point to some ways that many people can, a little piece at a time, build protection for themselves and their families and succeed in getting the care they need in these uncertain times. From student insurance to prescriptions to Medicare, if a reader is helped by only a few of the suggestions, I will have succeeded.

Figure 12

Worksheet: Making the Most of Flexible Savings Accounts

Out-of-pocket medical and dental expenses	Last year (actual)		Next year (estimated)
GENERAL CARE			
Premiums	Not eligible	Premiums	Not eligible
Deductible	$	Average actual deductible payment over past three years (last year if major change in medical condition)	$
Office visits (copayment/coinsurance)	$	Estimate baseline visits per year times out-of-pocket cost	$
Procedures (copayment/coinsurance)	$	Average actual copayment/ coinsurance payment over past three years (last year if major change in medical condition)	$
Hospital fees	$	Continuing treatment?	$
Lab and X-ray fees (medical)	$	Continuing treatment?	$
MEDICATIONS			
Premiums	Not eligible	Premiums	Not eligible
Deductible for prescription plan	$	Average actual deductible payment over past three years (last year if major change in medical condition)	$
Prescription drug copayments/coinsurance	$	Prescription drug copayments/coinsurance	$
Noncovered prescription drugs	$	Noncovered prescription drugs	$
Over-the-counter drugs (excluding items such as dietary supplements and sunscreens)	$	Over-the-counter drugs (excluding items such as dietary supplements and sunscreens)	$
Flu shots and other vaccinations	$	Flu shots and other vaccinations	$
VISION CARE			
Premiums	Not eligible	Premiums	Not eligible
Deductible for vision plan	$	Average actual deductible payment over past three years (last year if major change in medical condition)	$
Glasses (prescription)	$	Glasses (prescription)	$
Contact lenses	$	Contact lenses	$
Laser eye surgery	$	Expected next year?	$

Out-of-pocket medical and dental expenses	Last year (actual)		Next year (estimated)
HEARING CARE			
Hearing care	$	Hearing care	$
Hearing aids	$	Hearing aids	$
Batteries	$	Batteries	$
DENTAL CARE			
Premiums	Not eligible	Premiums	Not eligible
Deductible for dental plan	$	Average actual deductible payment over past three years (last year if major change in medical condition)	$
Office visits (copayments/coinsurance)	$	Office visits (copayments/coinsurance)	$
Surgery (copayments/coinsurance)	$	Continuing treatment?	$
Dentures and bridges	$	Dentures and bridges	$
Fillings and crowns	$	Fillings and crowns	$
Orthodontia	$	Continuing treatment?	$
OTHER (noncovered portions, including deductibles)			
Acupuncture	$	Continuing treatment?	$
Chiropractor	$	Continuing treatment?	$
Counseling/therapy	$	Continuing treatment?	$
Occupational therapy	$	Continuing treatment?	$
Physical therapy	$	Continuing treatment?	$
Wheelchairs and repairs	$	Continuing treatment?	$
Other	$	Continuing treatment?	$
TOTAL plan year election	$	**TOTAL plan year election**	$

SAVINGS IN FSA

Federal tax rate		%	
State tax rate (if applicable) +		%	
Total estimated tax rate =		% x Total plan year election =	$

Figure 13

Worksheet: Choosing the Health Plan for You

Your family medical status (including preexisting conditions):

Expected medical expense needs:

☐ Relatively healthy

☐ Hospitalization, surgery, or ongoing medical / lab treatments

☐ Frequent doctor's office visits

☐ Brand-name drug treatments

☐ Chronic medical condition

☐ Other: _____

Your primary goals:

☐ Low premium

☐ Low deductible

☐ Copayments rather than coinsurance

☐ Prescription drug coverage with low copay / coinsurance

☐ Low out-of-pocket annual maximum / high lifetime benefit cap

☐ Other: _____

Location 1:

Your Home State	HMO A	HMO B	PPO A	PPO B	HSA A	HSA B
Monthly premium	$	$	$	$	$	$
x 12 =						
Annual premium	$	$	$	$	$	$
Annual deductible +	$	$	$	$	$ *	$ *
Annual cost baseline (premium + deductible)	$	$	$	$	$	$
Scope of benefits:						
Copay (if applicable)	$	$	$	$	$	$
Coinsurance (if appl.)	$	$	$	$	$	$
Prescription drug coverage:						
Your medicines covered?	Yes No	Yes No	Yes No	Yes No	Yes No	Yes No
Copay (if applicable)	$	$	$	$	$	$
Coinsurance (if appl.)	$	$	$	$	$	$
Out-of-pocket maximum, after deductible	$	$	$	$	$	$
Lifetime benefit cap	$	$	$	$	$	$

Location 2:
Neighboring State

	HMO A	HMO B	PPO A	PPO B	HSA A	HSA B
Monthly premium	$	$	$	$	$	$
x 12 =						
Annual premium	$	$	$	$	$	$
Annual deductible +	$	$	$	$	$ *	$ *
Annual cost baseline (premium + deductible)	$	$	$	$	$	$

Scope of benefits:

	HMO A	HMO B	PPO A	PPO B	HSA A	HSA B
Copay (if applicable)	$	$	$	$	$	$
Coinsurance (if appl.)	$	$	$	$	$	$

Prescription drug coverage:

	HMO A	HMO B	PPO A	PPO B	HSA A	HSA B
Your medicines covered?	Yes No	Yes No	Yes No	Yes No	Yes No	Yes No
Copay (if applicable)	$	$	$	$	$	$
Coinsurance (if appl.)	$	$	$	$	$	$
Out-of-pocket maximum, after deductible	$	$	$	$	$	$
Lifetime benefit cap	$	$	$	$	$	$

Worksheet: Calculating the Value of an HSA

Federal tax rate		State tax rate (if applicable)		Total estimated tax rate
%	+	%	=	%

HSA annual funding amount   x $

*Match to an amount up to the policy's deductible (maximum of $2,700 per year for an individual, or $5,450 per year for a family)

HSA annual tax savings   = $

Figure 14

Worksheet: Cutting Prescription Drug Costs

Prescription 1:

	Pharmacy A:		Pharmacy B:		Pharmacy C:	
	30-day supply cost	Shipping if any	30-day supply cost	Shipping if any	30-day supply cost	Shipping if any
Price at prescribed dosage	$	$	$	$	$	$
Can the pill be split?	Yes	No				
Subtract price at twice the dosage ÷ 2	$	$	$	$	$	$
Savings	$	$	$	$	$	$

Prescription 2:

	Pharmacy A:		Pharmacy B:		Pharmacy C:	
	30-day supply cost	Shipping if any	30-day supply cost	Shipping if any	30-day supply cost	Shipping if any
Price at prescribed dosage	$	$	$	$	$	$
Can the pill be split?	Yes	No				
Subtract price at twice the dosage ÷ 2	$	$	$	$	$	$
Savings	$	$	$	$	$	$

Prescription 3:

	Pharmacy A:		Pharmacy B:		Pharmacy C:	
	30-day supply cost	Shipping if any	30-day supply cost	Shipping if any	30-day supply cost	Shipping if any
Price at prescribed dosage	$	$	$	$	$	$
Can the pill be split?	Yes	No				
Subtract price at twice the dosage ÷ 2	$	$	$	$	$	$
Savings	$	$	$	$	$	$

Prescription 4:	Pharmacy A:		Pharmacy B:		Pharmacy C:	
	30-day supply cost	Shipping if any	30-day supply cost	Shipping if any	30-day supply cost	Shipping if any
Price at prescribed dosage	$	$	$	$	$	$
Can the pill be split?	Yes	No				
Subtract price at twice the dosage ÷ 2	$	$	$	$	$	$
Savings	$	$	$	$	$	$

Prescription Log

	Prescription 1	Prescription 2
Name		
Dosage		
Frequency		
Rx date		
Number of refills		
End of Rx date		
Filled by pharmacy		
Pharmacy phone		
Checked Rx interactions		

	Prescription 3	Prescription 4
Name		
Dosage		
Frequency		
Rx date		
Number of refills		
End of Rx date		
Filled by pharmacy		
Pharmacy phone		
Checked Rx interactions		

Figure 15

Health Care and Insurer Log

Date	Provider (doctor, hospital, insurer)	Spoke to (name / title)	Services provided / received	Case number (if applicable)	Further action

Afterword: A New Framework

In a departure from the format of my previous books, I would like to end this book with a look at how the United States might tackle the big picture of health costs and the uninsured. It's a pragmatic decision. Although these policy issues will not make your health-care budget easier to manage in the next few years, you can influence your political representatives as they consider options. And some options will be much better for your wallet in the long run.

What is clearly needed is a new framework for health insurance that is universal and does not allow those with preexisting conditions to be excluded from coverage. The framework, however, must at the same time protect insurance companies from the financial consequences of adverse selection. Three proposals for change—one involving Medicare for all discussed in chapter 8, one from the 1970s, and another from the Century Foundation's Leif Haase—would do just that. The first and third would totally break the link between insurance and employment; the second would leave a small, voluntary role for employers. All have the potential to reduce spending on health care.

It was nearly thirty years after President Harry S. Truman failed to pass universal coverage in 1945 before another proposal for such coverage gained political traction. In 1972, Senator Russell B. Long, a Louisiana Democrat and chairman of the Senate Finance Committee, presented a plan for federal catastrophic health insurance. Although it enjoyed bipartisan support, Congress never passed it.

Under the Long plan, the government would pay all medical costs above an annual deductible of $2,000 for anyone not covered by Medicare. (Adjusted for inflation, that deductible today would be more like $8,000 to $10,000.) Insurance companies would underwrite much of the government's coverage. In addition, insurers could sell individual policies covering the deductible portion. For people who couldn't afford the deductible or insurance for it, Medicaid would pay.

It's difficult to find much wrong with the Long plan. Its big attraction is that it protects people from bankruptcy and from losing their homes or other property in the event of a catastrophic illness; it is also a boon for people who want to retire but are too young to qualify for Medicare and whose employers do not provide retirees with health benefits. The proposal includes participation by private insurance companies—which have a strong interest in the outcome of the debate over coverage. And it covers everyone: People at higher income levels have a choice of paying the deductible themselves, buying insurance for it, or seeking coverage provided by their employers; the poor would have their deductible covered by Medicaid. Because insurance companies' exposure for the deductible would be limited to paying a relatively small, capped amount each year, such policies would be much less expensive than the conventional ones offered today. And because costs would be low, small businesses would be encouraged to offer deductible coverage to their workers.

Such catastrophic insurance would for the most part avoid the bureaucracy that many people, rightly or wrongly, fear with national health insurance because most Americans would be unlikely ever to use it. According to the U.S. Agency for Healthcare Research and Quality, the average annual health-care expenses for people under age sixty-five, including payments by insurance carriers, was $2,138 in 2002; in the 1970s, that figure was less than $500. For people over age sixty-five, who usually have the biggest medical expenses, coverage would continue to be provided by Medicare.

Senator Long may have been "ahead of his time," according to Dr. James J. Mongan, the chief executive of Partners HealthCare System in Boston; his plan was certainly the victim of two Washington scandals that had nothing to do with health care: Watergate and the Fannie Fox stripper scandal that derailed much of the legislation in the House Ways and Means Committee under the chairmanship of Wilbur D. Mills. Jay Constantine, who worked for the Senate Finance Committee in the 1970s when Senator Long was chairman, pointed out that the catastrophic plan was good for its time and would be good today. "It would empower people," he said. "It would give them health care separate from corporations or their employers. This is especially important in the kind of mobile society we have now. It is the right track and the least costly approach to getting everybody covered." Alice M. Rivlin, a senior fellow at the Brookings Institution who is a former Federal Reserve governor and former director of the Office of Management and Budget, thinks such a catastrophic plan ought to be revived since it could hold down costs, especially among the population that pays the deductible themselves. But Rivlin wonders how popular the Long plan would be with the general public. "Americans are a bit irrational about health care," she said. "They like first-dollar coverage; they like to have all their health care covered rather than thinking of insurance as protection against large expenditures."

During the 2004 presidential election, there was a faint echo of Senator Long's 1972 catastrophic health insurance plan. The Democratic candidate, Senator John Kerry of Massachusetts, proposed that the government reimburse employers for 75 percent of any medical bills in excess of $50,000 that a worker ran up in a year. That proposal basically makes the government a secondary insurer to ease the pressure of insurance costs on employers and workers. While the plan also required employers who took advantage of the program to offer insurance to every worker, it would not have resulted in universal coverage like the Long plan.

While a classic single-payer, government-run health system like Canada's ensures that everyone is covered equally, Leif Haase of the Century Foundation does not think such a system would ever take hold in the United States. "Systems like Canada's are under enormous strain because under them, medical successes and new technology can have trouble becoming available rapidly, uniformly, and comprehensively," he said. Such systems also carry the stigma, fairly or unfairly, of rationed care, long waits for elective procedures, and bureaucracy. As we have seen, of course, these problems also can plague private insurance plans.

Traditional U.S. fee-for-service Medicare—which is, of course, essentially a single-payer, government-run system—is much more efficient than private insurance, with administrative costs at about 2 percent. In addition, the sheer size of a single-payer system like Medicare allows it to take advantage of economies of scale unavailable to a single private insurer. But given America's embrace of freedom of choice, polarized politics, and a Congress that is highly responsive to well-financed special-interest groups, Haase is probably correct. He argues that "we are moving toward a hybrid system that involves both the government and private insurers."

Haase has proposed a plan for universal coverage that, among other changes, would get employers out of the health insurance business and would eventually eliminate government health programs like Medicaid, Medicare, and the Veterans Health Administration. The federal government would subsidize individual and family purchase of private health insurance policies, with older, poorer, and disabled Americans receiving larger payments. He believes his proposal could, within a decade, become the foundation of a new American national health insurance program. His plan, titled *A New Deal for Health: How to Cover Everyone and Get Medical Costs Under Control,* was published in May 2005 by the Century Foundation and is available on the foundation's Web site (www.tcf.org).

Here are the principal elements of the Haase plan.

- The federal government would establish three levels of insurance coverage—basic, medium, and higher end—and would negotiate with private insurers over premiums and rules, much as it does for the rules on Medigap policies. Insurers could offer a menu of plans including, for instance, restricted physician networks or copayments. Insurers must, however, offer all three tiers of coverage if they offer any, and they may not pay different amounts to providers for medical procedures based on a patient's level of coverage. Each of the three plans must also include preventive care, as well as dental and vision coverage, which are rarely included in bare-bones plans sometimes available today for those on a very limited budget.
- The purchase of basic-level health insurance would be mandatory (much like that of liability insurance by drivers). Government subsidies based on income would make insurance coverage affordable for everyone.
- Insurance companies would not be allowed to reject applicants because of preexisting medical conditions.
- Medicare, Medicaid, and other government programs would be phased out. Current Medicare beneficiaries would have the option of joining the new national health program or staying with Medicare.
- There would be new investments in the public health system to encourage Americans to practice healthier lifestyles.
- An independent board would evaluate the cost-effectiveness of medical procedures and assess new technologies.

- The federal tax subsidy for employer-based insurance would be phased out. Employers would no longer be able to deduct the cost of health insurance from their taxes. The new revenues from eliminating this tax subsidy would pay a portion of the financing for Haase's proposal.
- Additional funding for the program would come from a payroll tax, a dedicated corporate tax, and general revenues.

The concept of mandatory health insurance is not new. As noted in chapter 1, everyone over age sixty-five is required to pay for Medicare Part A, which pays for hospital bills. In an interview for my January 2003 "Seniority" column in the *New York Times*, then-Senator John Breaux, a conservative Louisiana Democrat, called for universal mandatory coverage that shared some features of the Haase plan because, he said, "the American health-care system is collapsing around us." According to Breaux: "In our current system, we have all these boxes. If you're old, you're in the Medicare box. If you're a veteran, you're in the V.A. box. If you're working, you're in the employer-sponsored box. Each of these boxes has a huge bureaucracy and spends a lot of money. We need to get people out of these boxes that don't make a lot of sense. What we ought to say is that if you're an American citizen, you have to buy health insurance, just like drivers have to have liability insurance. But this insurance should come from the private sector and not be a single-payer plan. I would not support a government-run program. We just can't micromanage health care that way." He emphasized that the government would subsidize premiums, depending on an individual's income, and that no one should be denied coverage or be forced to pay higher rates because of preexisting conditions. Unlike the Haase plan, however, Breaux—who has continued to work on behalf of health-care reform through his bipartisan Ceasefire on Health Care campaign since retiring from the Senate—would not break the link between employers and employee health care; companies could continue to pay the premiums for their workers.

That's an important difference, because a lot of companies would like to get out of the health-care business. Haase believes, along with Stephen Wyss of Affinity Group Underwriters, that the extra taxes companies might pay to shed employee coverage would be less expensive and more predictable than the amounts they are now spending for employee health care.

Further, Haase contends that his plan would maintain the existing relationship between doctors, insurers, and patients; preserve U.S. leadership in medical innovation; and allow Americans to see the doctors of their choice. "The positive aspects of our current system should be retained," he explained. "In many respects, this plan resembles the way congressmen get their current coverage. It would be financed in much the same way that today's system is financed, and for only a modest additional cost."

Haase suggests that his plan is flexible enough to incorporate other reform proposals, such as the Long catastrophic health insurance proposal, to extend its coverage. According to Haase, the Long plan was "ingenious" and included "a lot of individual responsibility, but on the front end [in the form of deductibles] instead of on the back end [in the form of payment caps]."

A big plus for the Haase plan is that it appeals to the middle of the political spectrum, an approach long urged by Breaux. It combines elements of a single-payer system—mandatory universal coverage and regulated benefits—favored by liberals, with free-market elements—private insurance and choice—favored by conservatives. The plan also fills the two gaping holes in our present system: affordability and coverage for people with preexisting conditions. It would also lessen the problem of adverse selection—although not as much as a single-payer plan—because companies would insure the entire country and lose the ability to cherry-pick or reject people with preexisting conditions.

Haase believes it is better for the federal government to establish single standards for coverage rather than have a confusing array of standards, depending on individual insurance companies and state laws. Another plus he sees in his plan is that it would eliminate Medicaid and eventually Medicare. "Medicaid deserves to be replaced," he said. "It's a program of arbitrary eligibility, based on whatever the sensibilities of the politicians in a particular state are at a particular time. And, in reality, you often can't get a doctor to treat you if you are under Medicaid. This is beginning to happen to Medicare. Medicare is to some degree going down the Medicaid path. That ought to be a big concern to seniors and the disabled."

Haase's plan calls for mandatory coverage—but what if you wait to buy insurance until you are sick, then cancel when you are well? After all, there are plenty of drivers who flout laws requiring them to have liability insurance. Haase has a response: "I think that would be a pretty small problem that wouldn't sink a national plan like this. People would see the value of having insurance, especially if subsidies make it affordable for them."

Haase sees a growing constituency for changes and thinks employers and corporations will eventually get behind a plan like his. "There is enormous dissatisfaction and unhappiness about health care that is inchoate because Americans don't know whom to blame," he said. "They tend to blame, in turn, pharmaceutical companies and then managed care. It's, of course, a much bigger problem due to the history we have and the fact that our structures are no longer suited to trends in medicine and our expectations.

"The system has already failed and is in chaos. The actors who are running the system haven't fully acknowledged the failure. The tendency is to think we can keep patching up the problems. It's like an old car you're trying to get through another season."

ON THE WEB

In addition to the resources listed in this section, your own state's Web site is an important source of information on the insurance regulations that dictate the costs and benefits of your insurance.

www.aarp.org is the Web site for AARP, which has what may be the best collection of information on Medigap health insurance policies.

www.agu.net has some of the best and most current information on high-risk pools in the states that offer them. The site is run by Affinity Group Underwriters.

www.ahia.net, the Web site of the Association of Health Insurance Advisors, helps you find an independent health insurance agent in your area.

www.ambest.com is the site for the information clearinghouse A. M. Best Company, which, among other things, rates insurance companies.

www.ameriplanusa.com is the site of AmeriPlan USA, which sells health discount cards. Don't confuse the discount cards with health insurance.

www.borgdrug.com is run by Borg Drug (in Ashby, Minnesota), which is one of the most inexpensive places in the United States to buy prescription drugs (see chapter 6). Borg Drug sells drugs at near-wholesale cost. The Web site lists drug prices and information about ordering through the mail or over the phone.

www.cahi.org is the Web site for the Council for Affordable Health Insurance, an advocacy group for insurers, where you can find an up-to-date list of state mandates for health coverage. From the home page, click on "Publications & Resources."

www.canadapharmacy.com is a site for buying prescription drugs from Canada (see chapter 6). It's operated by Canada Pharmacy.

www.careington.com is another company that sells health discount cards—again, not to be confused with health insurance.

www.claims.org is operated by the Alliance of Claims Assistance Professionals, which helps consumers find professionals who, for a fee, will help with insurance claims. The group also provides help to those who wish to become claims assistance professionals.

www.ConsumerReports.org is *the* site, although it's not free, for coping with a wide range of consumer issues and questions, including advice on various kinds of health insurance.

www.costco.com is Costco's Internet shopping site, where you can price and purchase prescription drugs at prices that are among the lowest in this country.

www.cvs.com is the site for CVS, the drugstore chain.

www.drugstore.com is a big online drugstore.

www.ehealthinsurance.com is an online health insurance broker. At eHealthInsurance.com you can buy health insurance or just get the lowdown on prices and what's available in the various states. The company is a major player in marketing health savings accounts.

www.familiesusa.org is the Web site of Families USA, a nonprofit health-care advocacy group that seeks affordable health care for all.

www.healthclaimassistance.net is the site of a Chicago company, Health Claim Assistance, which for a fee helps people file and manage health insurance claims.

www.healthinsuranceinfo.net is the site for the Georgetown University Health Policy Institute, a source for current information on health insurance in various states.

www.howstuffworks.com is a great site for curious people. It contains some health-related information, including sections on "how health insurance works" and "how Medicare works."

www.hsainsider.com provides insurance industry information on health savings accounts.

www.iiaa.org, run by the Independent Insurance Agents and Brokers of America, can help you find a health insurance agent.

www.kff.org, which is operated by the Kaiser Family Foundation, is a key source of comprehensive, nonpartisan health-care data. The Web site reviews consumer protections as well as average costs, state-by-state and nationally, for both employer-sponsored and individual insurance.

www.kff.org/consumerguide provides a very useful resource list for appealing the rejection of a health insurance claim, whether you live in a state with external review or not.

www.MedBasketMexico.com is for those who want to order prescription drugs from Mexico.

www.medicare.gov is a consumer-oriented site run by the Center for Medicare and Medicaid Services. It contains very helpful and detailed information on the latest Medicare rules, as well as the benefits offered by Medicare Part B and Part D.

www.medicarerights.org is the site of the Medicare Rights Center, a nonprofit group that helps people with Medicare questions and problems.

www.nahu.org, the site of the National Association of Health Underwriters, can help you find an independent health insurance agent.

www.naic.org is run by the National Association of Insurance Commissioners. It can help with insurance regulations in the various states.

www.phrma.org can be of assistance if you're trying to get free prescription drugs from a pharmaceutical company. The Pharmaceutical Research and Manufacturers of America runs the site.

www.prescriptions4free.com is another site that can help you, for a fee, in getting free drugs from manufacturers. Harson Hill runs it.

www.racinereport.com is operated by the *Racine Journal Times* in Racine, Wisconsin. Dustin Block, the city editor, uses the site to provide health-care news and a forum for people who are underinsured or have no coverage. Type in "health care" and click on the search button.

www.savvysenior.org is the Web site of Jim Miller, whose column, "The Savvy Senior," runs in hundreds of small daily and weekly newspapers around the country. On the site you can read his columns, in which he often deals with Medicare and health-related issues. You can also send him questions.

www.tcf.org is the site operated by the Century Foundation, a non-profit group that does a lot of work on health-care issues.

www.walgreens.com is the drugstore chain's Web site.

www.walmart.com is the retailer's Web site, where you can access information about its pharmacy services.

OFF THE SHELF

Critical Condition: How Health Care in America Became Big Business and Bad Medicine (Doubleday, 2004), by Donald L. Barlett and James B. Steel. A stunning and frightening exposé of the American health-care system's shortcomings by two of the country's top investigative reporters.

The $800 Million Pill: The Truth Behind the Cost of New Drugs (University of California Press, 2004), by Merrill Goozner. Why do prescription drugs cost so much? Hint: It's not because drug companies spend so much money on research.

The European Dream: How Europe's Vision of the Future Is Quietly Eclipsing the American Dream (Jeremy P. Tarcher/Penguin, 2004), by Jeremy Rifkin. An eye-opening read for those who are smug about the American way of life.

The New Health Insurance Solution: How to Get Cheaper, Better Coverage Without a Traditional Employer Plan (John Wiley & Sons, 2005), by Paul Zane Pilzer. A fairly helpful, detailed book. It is, however, a little too hopeful about health savings accounts and a little too dismissive of the problems of people with preexisting conditions.

One Nation Uninsured: Why the U.S. Has No National Health Insurance (Oxford University Press, 2005), by Jill Quadagno. A fine and readable history of how we got where we are.

The Pill Book, 12th edition (Bantam, 2006), by Harold M. Silverman. This handy, often-updated reference for nonprofessionals includes descriptions of drug interactions to help you juggle prescriptions filled by multiple pharmacies. Keep in mind that you should also consult your doctor and can ask for help from your pharmacist, whether you go to one drugstore or not for all of your prescriptions.

Profit Is Not the Cure: A Citizen's Guide to Saving Medicare (McClelland & Stewart, 2002), by Maude Barlow. *Medicare* in the subtitle refers not to the U.S. program for the elderly but to the Canadian system of universal care. The book is a cogent argument against efforts to reintroduce privatized medicine to Canada.

Uninsured in America: Life and Death in the Land of Opportunity (University of California Press, 2005), by Susan Starr Sered and Rushika Fernandopulle. This book argues that the link between health insurance and employment is creating a new caste in America of the ill, infirm, and marginally employed. The profiles of people without insurance are tragic and touching.

You: The Smart Patient: An Insider's Guide to Getting the Best Treatment (Free Press, 2006), by Michael F. Roizen and Mehmet C. Oz. This second book by the best-selling author of *You: The Owner's Manual* offers tips for being better informed about your medical condition and includes sample forms for recording personal and family medical histories.

acknowledgments

I would like to thank all the people who agreed to be interviewed for this book and were often willing to discuss private details of their medical lives. I am especially indebted to Brenda Surin, Nancy Dennis, Henry Hamman, and Richard Price. Thanks to Emily Fox of eHealthInsurance.com for never failing to track down answers to my many questions about health insurance. Thanks also to the patient people in the press office at the Centers for Medicare and Medicaid Services, as well as a couple of insurance industry sources whose names I have agreed not to disclose.

A very special thanks to Alice Martell, my agent who is always there for me; the *New York Times*'s Pat Lyons, who created the graphics for this book as well as my previous two books; and Vicki Haire, my talented copy editor. I would also like to thank my colleagues in the A. Q. Miller School of Journalism and Mass Communications at Kansas State University and Angela Powers, the director, for their help and kindness.

Finally, I am grateful to my wife, Evelyn, whose advice—editorial and otherwise—is always on target.

index

Aaron, Henry J., 18, 69, 162
AARP, 122, 139, 182
Adler, David, 92
adverse selection, 24, 77, 92, 110, 187, 192
Affinity Group Underwriters, 110
Alliance of Claims Assistance Professionals, 158
Altman, Drew E., 34–35
A. M. Best Company, 173
American Hospital Association, 53
American Journal of Cardiology, 129
American Medical Association, 18
AmeriPlan USA, 114
amyotrophic lateral sclerosis (Lou Gehrig's disease), 162
Anderson, Gerard F., 14–15
Antos, Joseph, 73
appealing claim rejections, 148, 150
appeals process, 150
success in, 152
Archer, Diane, 159, 166–67, 174–75
Arizona Republic, 23
associated health plans, 191–92
Associated Press, 51
Association of Health Insurance Advisors, 118
associations, health care offered through, 109, 117
attorneys, hiring to negotiate a hospital bill, 54

baby boomers
Medicare and, 1
political clout of, 68–69
Baldwin, Tammy, 72
bankruptcies, personal, 7, 10
the insured and, 35–38, 39
Long plan and, 202
Beach, Richard, 177, 179–80
Beebe, Deane, 137, 169
Block, Dustin, 31
Borg Drug, 119–22, 123, 125–28
Boston University, 13, 14
Breaux, John B., 1, 23, 206
brokers, insurance, 104, 118
Burger, Deborah, 50
Bush, George W., 71, 77
BusinessWeek, 23

California HealthCare Foundation, 51
Canada
buying prescription drugs from, 130–33, 138, 192
health-care system, 23–24, 25, 27–29, 204
Canada Pharmacy, 130–33
Caraway, Jeanine, 116–18
Careington, 114
CBS Evening News, 119–21
Ceasefire on Health Care campaign, 23, 206
Center for Pharmacoeconomic Studies, University of Texas at Austin, 133

Centers for Medicare and Medicaid Services, 164, 165
Century Foundation proposal to universal coverage, 201, 204–8
cherry-picking, 24, 187, 188
Chicago Tribune, 68
childbirth, maternal deaths in, 6
children
    Medicaid eligibility, 108
    uninsured, 5–6
CIA World Factbook, 3–4
cities, most affordable for buying health insurance, 104–6
Civil Society Institute, 23
claims assistance professional (CAP), hiring a, 157–58
Clinton, Bill, 20
Clinton, Hillary Rodham, 145
COBRA (Consolidated Omnibus Budget Reconciliation Act), 61–63, 96, 116–17
    application period, 62
    case study, 63–67
    costs of coverage, 62, 96
    HIPAA and. *See* HIPAA (Health Insurance Portability and Accountability Act)
    preexisting conditions and, 61
    premiums, 62, 96
    short-term insurance after, 109
    spousal coverage, 61–62
coinsurance, 35, 52
    defined, 40
    Medicare, 163, 164
    for prescription drugs, 122
collection agencies, 39
college students, coverage for, 111–13
commissions, insurance broker, 104
Commonwealth Fund, 6–7, 9, 25, 37, 39, 67, 89
complicated claims, rejection or delay in payment of, 153
concierge practices, 26
Consolidated Omnibus Budget Reconciliation Act. *See* COBRA (Consolidated Omnibus Budget Reconciliation Act)
Constantine, Jay, 203
consumer-driven health care, 21, 71, 175, 187
    health savings accounts. *See* health savings accounts (HSAs)

coordination of benefits, 45, 190
copayments, 35, 38
    defined, 40–42
    Medicare Advantage plans, 167
    for prescription drugs, 122
Costco, 123, 124–25
costs of health care
    difficulty in comparing prices, 72–73
    health access problems related to, 8
    hospital charges. *See* hospital charges and billing
    international comparisons, 13–15
    methods of coping with, 39–41
    per capita, 47
    reasonable and customary charges, 147, 150–51
    rising, 3, 7, 23, 34, 35, 40, 59
    see also specific costs, e.g., out-of-pocket expenses; premiums, insurance
Council for Affordable Health Insurance, 102–3
credit for prior coverage, defined, 42
CVS, 125–28

Davis, Karen, 89
Deal, Nathan, 72
deductibles, 35, 38
    defined, 42
    high-deductible plans. *See* high-deductible plans
    Medicare, 163, 164
defensive medicine, 14
delays in resolving insurance claims, 153
Dennis, George and Nancy, 54–57, 153
dental coverage, 165
    discount clubs and, 113–14
dialysis treatments, 19, 162
DiamondCluster International, 91
diary, health care. *See* recordkeeping
disabled
    Medicaid coverage for, 108
    Medicare coverage for, 25, 162
discount clubs and cards, 113–14, 134–35
doctors
    changing, 177–80, 181
    discount clubs, doctor bills and, 113–14
    mistakes in bills from, 153–54
    unexpected out-of-network charges, 147, 152
Dressler, Susan A., 156, 157–58
drug companies
    executive compensation, 50

free drugs from, 141–42
profits, 49
drugs, prescription. *See* prescription drugs
Drugstore.com, 123–24, 125–28

eHealthInsurance, 75, 76, 79, 83, 88, 99, 103–4, 114
elective procedures, waiting period for, 14, 25–26, 204
emergency rooms
plan coverage for services in, 148
treatment of uninsured, 11, 50, 50*n*, 175
waiting period for treatment, 25–26
Empire Blue Cross Blue Shield of New York, 166
Employee Benefit Research Institute, 10, 39–40, 59, 73, 89
employer-based insurance, x, 1, 32, 96
benefits coordinators, assistance from, 157
businesses, financial effects on, 3, 19–20
Clinton's plan, 20
COBRA and, 61–63
collapse of, 21, 22, 59, 178, 187–88
decline in companies offering, 34–35, 59
Haase proposal for universal health care and, 206–7
health savings accounts, 44, 75, 79–81, 86, 189
illness and loss of insurance, 96
insured or self-funded, 147–48
job hopping and, 27
job lock and, 3, 60, 61
open-enrollment period, annual, 189
origins of, 17, 19–20, 59
ranking of importance as job-related benefit, 59–60
sorting out your options, 188–91
statistics, 22, 59
switching of plans by companies, 178–79
EOB (explanation of benefits), 51–52
carefully studying, value of, 145–46
defined, 42
recordkeeping, 150
EPO (exclusive provider organization) plan
defined, 42
Errors, medical, 7
Evensky & Katz, 80, 81
excluded services, 148

explanation of benefits. *See* EOB (explanation of benefits)

Fahlman, Robert, 81–82
Families USA, 9, 10, 11, 12, 107, 108, 123
family coverage. *See specific types of health care coverage, e.g.,* employer-based insurance; individual health insurance
family medical history, long-term care insurance and, 184
fee-for-service (indemnity) plans, 44, 148, 189
defined, 42
Fernandopulle, Rushika, 31–32
fine-print limits, 46
flexible spending accounts (FSAs), 76–77, 181, 191
worksheet, 194–95
fraud, 13
free-drug programs, 141–42
Friedman, Saul, 135
FSAs (flexible spending accounts), 76–77

General Motors, health-care costs of, 3, 178
generic drugs. *See* prescription drugs
Georgetown University Health Policy Institute, 98
Great Britain, health-care system in, 17
guaranteed-issue laws, states with, 96–97, 98, 102, 110, 167–68, 191
map of, 111
Guillain-Barré syndrome, 56

Haase, Leif Wellington, 17, 19–20, 21, 22
proposal to universal coverage, 201, 204–8
Haggar Corporation, 116
Hamman, Henry, 59, 63–67
Harris Interactive polls, 23
Harson Hill, 142
Hartke, Vance, 19
Harvard Law School, 7
Harvard Medical School, 7
Harvard School of Public Health, 39, 53–54
Hayes, Robert M., 18–19, 159, 160, 168
Health Affairs, 14
Health Care Payers Coalition of New Jersey, 49
Health Claim Assistance, 158
Health Insurance Portability and Accountability Act. *See* HIPAA (Health Insurance Portability and Accountability Act)

health maintenance organizations (HMOs),
    5, 20, 148, 189–90
    COBRA coverage and, 62
    defined, 42–43
    executive compensation, 50
    Medicare Advantage program, 165–68
    privatizing of Medicare and, 161, 162
    profits of, 49
"Health of Nations: Medicine and the Free
    Market," 21
health savings accounts (HSAs), x, 20–21,
    71–93, 181, 188
    availability of, 75
    control factor, 79–80
    defined, 43
    determining suitability of, 86–91
    employers offering, 44, 75, 79–81, 86, 189
    example, for family of four, 84–86
    fees, 91
    flexible spending accounts (FSAs)
        distinguished from, 76–77
    high-deductible plans and, 47, 68, 72,
        73–76, 77, 79, 80, 83–84, 189
    how they work, 73–76
    investment value, 74, 91
    legislation creating, 71
    maximum annual contributions to, 74
    penalties, 74
    preexisting conditions and, 75, 77–78,
        82–83
    premiums, 76, 78, 84
    pros and cons of, 77–79
    South Africa's experience with, 92
    tax implications, 74, 75, 77, 86, 181
    worksheet to calculate value of, 197
    for young adults, 82–84
high-deductible plans, x
    health savings accounts and, 47, 68, 72,
        73–76, 77, 79, 80, 83–84, 189
high-risk pool, 110, 111
Himmelstein. David, 10, 31
HIPAA (Health Insurance Portability and
    Accountability Act), 62–63, 66, 117
    application period, 63
    costs of, 63
    preexisting condition and, 63
    short-term insurance prior to, 109
history of health care in the U.S., 17–22
HMOs. See health maintenance
    organizations (HMOs)
hospital charges and billing, 47–50, 72–73, 158
    charge master, 51

discount clubs, 113–14
    insurance companies, rates for, 48
    itemized bill, demanding a, 53
    log of services received, 53
    negotiating, 50–54
    price inquiries, 51
    profits, 49, 53
    results of challenging, 149
hospitals included in plan's coverage, 148
house calls, 15
HSAs. See health savings accounts (HSAs)
Humana, 138, 166
Hurley, Robert, 74–75, 77–79, 97

indemnity plan. See fee-for-service
    (indemnity) plans
Independent Insurance Agents and Brokers
    of America, 118
individual health insurance, 61, 96, 188
    age and, 67–68
    cities, most affordable, 104–6
    COBRA and. See COBRA (Consolidated
        Omnibus Budget Reconciliation Act)
    community rating, 96, 98
    guaranteed-issue laws, states with, 96–97,
        98, 102, 110, 111, 191
    HIPAA and. See HIPAA (Health
        Insurance Portability and
        Accountability Act)
    preexisting conditions and, x, 96, 97
    shopping for, 99–104
    sorting out your options, 191–92
    state law and, 96–99, 188
infant mortality rates, international, 3–4
Ingenix, 151
Institute for Health and Socioeconomic
    Policy (IHSP), 49
insurance brokers, 104, 118
insurance claims, problems in resolving. See
    problems with insurance companies,
    avoiding or resolving
insurance companies, 17
    explanation of benefits from. See EOB
        (explanation of benefits)
    problems with, avoiding or resolving. See
        problems with insurance companies,
        avoiding or resolving
    ratings, 173
    special health-care coordinators at, 57
international comparisons of health-care
    systems, 3–5, 6–7, 8, 11, 13–16
    charts, 8, 16

origins of the systems, 17–18
waiting period for treatment, 25–26

job, health insurance through your. *See* employer-based insurance
Johnson, Lyndon B., 18, 162
Journal of the American Medical Association, 4, 5, 107

Kaiser Family Foundation, 1, 23, 34, 39, 53, 107–8, 110, 136, 152
Annual Employer Health Benefits Survey, 34
understanding your policy, Web site information to aid in, 147–48, 174
Kansas State University, 112
Katz, Deena, 80–82, 182–85
Kerry, John, 203–4
Kiplinger's retirement planning guide, 173
Kristof, Nicholas D., 4
Krugman, Paul, 137, 175

lawyers, hiring to negotiate hospital bills, 54
life expectancy at birth, international comparisons of, 4
lifetime maximum, 44–45, 84
defined, 43
of health savings accounts, 90
limited benefit plans, 46–47
Lipitor, 123–24
Live Well on Less Than You Think: The New York Times Guide to Achieving Your Financial Freedom (Brock), 181
logs, health care. *See* recordkeeping
Long, Russell B., proposal for universal health care, 202–3
long-term-care insurance, 182–85
Lou Gehrig's disease, 162

McKinsey & Company, 88
malpractice lawsuits, 14
managed care, 5, 21
Medicare Advantage plans, 165–68
privatizing of Medicare and, 161, 162
Manchin, Joe, 51
Massachusetts universal coverage law, 97
MedBasketMexico.com, 134
Medicaid, 1, 5, 106–8, 183, 192, 204, 208
children, coverage for, 6
creation of, 18

doctors refusing patients on, 107
eligibility for, 38, 106–8, 208
medical debt
bankruptcies. *See* bankruptcies, personal
statistics, 37, 39
Medicare, 9, 18, 24–25, 28, 159–75
administrative expenses, 161, 204
for all Americans, 174–75
amyotrophic lateral sclerosis (Lou Gehrig's disease), coverage of, 162
baby boomers and, 1
budget projections, 159–61
catastrophic coverage law, repeal of, 69
Clinton buy-in proposal, 20
coinsurance, 163, 164
creation of, 18, 162
deductibles, 163, 164
dialysis coverage, 19, 162
disabled, coverage of, 25, 38, 56, 162
facts, important, 162–65
financial soundness of, 159–61
hospital payments, 49, 53
Medicare Advantage program, 165–68, 174
Part A (hospital care), 25, 160, 163, 206
Part B (doctor bills and outpatient services), 160, 163, 166
Part D (prescription drug coverage), 19, 72, 123, 135–39, 141, 160, 163, 165, 169
popularity of, 162, 175
privatizing, attempts at, 160–61, 162
success of, 18–19
telephone number, 174
Web sites, helpful, 164, 174
see also Medigap policies
medicare.gov, 164, 174
Medicare private fee-for-service (PFFS) plan, 165
Medicare Rights Center, 137, 159, 164–65
medicarerights.org, 164–65
Medigap policies, 163, 165, 167
attained age pricing, 169, 173
chart, 170–71
community-rated pricing, 172, 173
issue age pricing, 169
Medicare Advantage plans compared to, 166, 167
overview of, 168–69, 170–71
per person pricing, 174
preexisting conditions, 166, 168, 174
premiums, 169–73, 174

Medigap policies (*cont'd*)
  ratings of insurance companies offering,
    173
  renewability of, 174
  six-month window, 166, 167, 174
  switching among, 174
  travel outside the U.S., 174
MEGA Life and Health Insurance
    Company, 112, 113, 117
Mercer Human Resource Consulting, 81
Mexico, buying prescription drugs from,
    133–34
Miami Herald, 125
Milwaukee Journal Sentinel, 51
"minimed" plans, 46–47
minority groups, 18
  disparity in health care, 7–8
mistakes in calculating your benefits, 147,
    153
Mongan, James J., 203
moral hazard theory, 71–73, 137

National Academy of Sciences, 6
National Association for the Self-Employed,
    117
National Association of Health
    Underwriters, 118
National Association of Insurance
    Commissioners, 98, 107, 182
national health insurance. *See* universal
    health-care coverage
National Institute of Neurological
    Disorders, 56
*New Deal for Health: How to Cover
    Everyone and Get Medical Costs Under
    Control, A,* 205–8
New Republic, 3, 21, 92, 93
New Yorker, 177
New York Times, 22, 26, 28, 72, 137, 157,
    175, 206
New York Times/CBS News polls, 23
Nissan, 178
nonparent adults, Medicaid eligibility of,
    108
NorthJersey.com, 48, 49
not medically necessary, services deemed,
    147, 152

Odle, Mary Lou, 183
One Nation, Uninsured (Quadagno), 18
Organization for Economic Cooperation
    and Development (OECD), 6

out-of-network charges, unexpected, 147,
    152
out-of-pocket expenses, 10
  flexible spending accounts (FSAs) and,
    76–77
  health savings accounts and, 78
  international comparisons, 7
  statistics, 35, 39
  switching doctors to lower, 54
  see also coinsurance; copayments;
    deductibles
out-of-pocket maximum, 44
  defined, 43

Palmer, John L., 159, 160
parents of dependent children, Medicaid
    eligibility of, 108
Parson, Mary H. "Jody," 185
Partnership for Prescription Assistance,
    142
payment caps on medical and surgical
    procedures, policies with, 46–47
Pear, Robert, 72
pensions, 177
PFFS, Medicare, 165
Pharmaceutical Research and
    Manufacturers of America, 141–42
Phillips, Rich, 79, 80
Physicians for a National Health Program
    (PNHP), 10
pills. *See* prescription drugs
pill-splitting, 128–30, 131, 192
point-of-service (POS) plan, 148
  defined, 43
political power, 68–69, 201
Pollack, Ron, 10
POS plan. *See* point-of-service (POS) plan
PPO. *See* preferred provider organization
    (PPO)
preexisting conditions, 22, 93, 187
  associated health plans and, 191–92
  changing insurers and coverage of, 55
  COBRA and, 61
  guaranteed-issue laws, states with, 96–97,
    98, 191
  health savings accounts and, 75, 77–78,
    82–83
  HIPAA and, 63
  individual insurance, qualifying for, x, 96,
    97
  long-term-care insurance, 185
  Medicaid and, 192

Medicare Advantage plans, 168
Medigap policies and, 166, 168, 174
reforming the system and, 23
short-term insurance and, 109
preferred provider organization (PPO), 84,
90, 148, 189–90
defined, 43–44
Medicare Advantage program, 165–68
pregnancy and prenatal care, 6
premiums, insurance, 10, 11–13, 27, 189–90
changing jobs and coverage of, 54–57
cities, most affordable, 104–6
employee contributions, 34, 178
employer's contribution, 34, 40, 178
examples of cheapest policies available,
99–102
guaranteed-issue states, 98–99, 102, 191
health savings accounts, 76, 78, 84
long-term-care insurance, 182, 183
Medigap policies, 169–73, 174
rising, 34, 35, 59
spouse's, 54–57, 190
state where you live, shopping for
individual policies and, 99–104
uninsured, hidden cost of paying for the,
11–13
prescription drugs, 119–43
buying from Canada, 130–33, 138, 192
buying from Mexico, 133–34
buying from more than one source,
tracking drug interactions and, 142–43
coinsurance for, 122
comparing prices, 124–28
copayments for, 122
discount clubs and cards, 113–14, 134–35
dosage and price, 123–24, 128–30
drug interactions, 142–43
employer cutbacks on drug coverage, 122
failure to fill prescriptions, 39
free drugs from pharmaceutical
companies, 141–42
health savings accounts and, 91
illogical retail prices, 122
Internet sources of, 54
markup on generic vs. brand-name drugs,
120, 192
Medicare, Part D, 19, 72, 123, 135–39,
141
rising costs of, 122–23
shipping charges, 127, 133
sorting out your options, 192
splitting pills, 128–30, 131, 192

state ranking by cost of an average
prescription, 139–41
strategies for lowering your costs, 124–39
wholesale prices, 120, 122–23
worksheet, 198–99
see also drug companies
Prevailing Healthcare Charges System, 151
preventive care, 77, 84
health savings accounts and, 91
Price, Richard, 145–46
primary-care system, 5, 11
financial pressures and failure to visit a
doctor, 39
high-deductibles and preventive care, 77
problems with insurance companies,
avoiding or resolving, 146–50
appealing, 148, 150
certified mail, 156
delays in calculating your benefits, 147,
153
hiring a claims assistance professional,
157–58
insurance company representatives,
dealing with, 149–50
knowledge about your coverage, essential,
147–48
medically necessary, service not deemed,
147, 152
mistakes in calculating your benefits, 147,
153
reasonable and customary (R&C),
charges, 147, 150–51
resolving disputes before paying bills,
154–56
unexpected out-of-network charges, 147,
152

Quadagno, Jill, 18

Racine Journal Times, 31
reasonable and customary charges, 147,
150–51
recordkeeping, 145–46, 149–50, 156, 181
bills, 150
claims, 150
EOBs, 150
health care and insurer log (form), 200
health-care providers, 149
hospital services received, log of, 53, 149
insurance company representatives,
conversations with, 149–50
tape recorder to aid in, 149

reforming the health-care system, 22–26
refunds, 154, 156
Relman, Arnold S., 3, 17, 21, 93
resources, 209–13
    books, 212–13
    on the Web, 209–12
retirement
    balancing costs and coverage of
        health-care plans, 180–81
    case studies, 179–80
    early, health insurance needs and, 60–61,
        68, 202–3
    employer-sponsored coverage in, 166
    long-term-care insurance, 182–85
    Medicare. See Medicare
    reducing spending in, 181
    saving for, 40, 178
Retire on Less Than You Think: The New
    York Times Guide to Planning Your
    Financial Future (Brock), 111
Rivlin, Alice, 203
Robert Wood Johnson Foundation, 5–6
Rostenkowski, Dan, 68–69

savings rate, U.S., 178
Sears, 178
secondary coverage, 45–46, 52, 190, 204
self-employed, 117–18
    uninsured, 10
self-funded employer policies, 147–48
Sered, Susan Starr, 31–32
shipping charges for prescription drugs,
    127, 133
shopping
    for individual health insurance policies,
        99–104
    for prescription drugs, 124–28
short-term insurance, 109
Slavitt, Andy, 81
small businesses
    health savings accounts and, 79–81
    offering health coverage, 34–35, 95
    start-ups, 61
    uninsured employees of, 10
smoking-cessation programs, 78
Social Security disability, 38, 56
South Africa, health savings accounts in, 92
specialists, 5
Starbucks, 3
Starfield, Barbara, 4–5, 25, 77
State Children's Health Insurance Program
    (SCHIP), 6

state insurance regulatory agencies, 148,
    153, 192
state where you live, relevance of, 95–118,
    188, 191
    cancellation provisions, 97
    case study, 114–16
    college and university students, coverage
        for, 111–13
    community rating, 96, 98
    guaranteed-issue laws, 96–97, 98, 102,
        110, 111, 167–68, 191
    health plan selection worksheet, 196–97
    high-risk pool, 110, 111
    long-term-care insurance, 183
    Medicaid eligibility and, 106–8
    ranking of states for healthfulness, 114–16
    rankings by cost of average prescription,
        139–41
    rate increases, 97–98
    shopping for insurance and, 99–104
    state mandates, 102–3
stop-loss, 44
    defined, 43
student health insurance, 36, 111–13
surgical procedures, policies with payment
    caps on, 46–47
Surin, Brenda, 35–38
Surowiecki, James, 177

taxes
    employer-based insurance and, 22
    health savings accounts and, 74, 75, 77,
        86, 181
    long-term-care insurance, state incentives
        and, 185
    national health-care systems and, 27
terminology of health insurance industry,
    40–44
Time Insurance, 113
travel outside the coverage area, plan
    stipulation on, 148
    Medicare Advantage plans, 167
    Medigap policies and travel outside the
        U.S., 174
Truman, Harry S., 18, 201

underinsured, the, 8–11
    statistics, 39
    stories of, 32–34
uninsured, the, 5, 8–11
    by age, 9
    children, 5–6

hidden costs in insurance premiums to
pay for, 11–13
hospital charges and, 48–49
statistics, ix, 1, 5, 9–10, 67, 82, 96, 187
working families, 10
young adults, 82–83
*Uninsured in America: Life and Death in
the Land of Opportunity* (Sered and
Fernandopulle), 31–32
unions, health benefits and, 81
United Health Foundation, 114
UnitedHealth Group, 151
United Nations, 6
U.S. Agency for Healthcare Research and
Quality, 34, 39, 40, 67, 123, 203
U.S. Census Bureau, 9, 10, 11
U.S. Commerce Department, 178
U.S. Customs, 132, 134
U.S. Department of the Treasury, 76
universal health-care coverage
Canadian system, 23–24, 25, 27–29
in Europe, 17–18
government role in, 28
Medicare coverage, expanding,
174–75
past U.S. attempts to create, 18–20, 201
proposals for, 174–75, 201–8
support for, 23
see also Medicaid; Medicare

University of California, 5
university students, coverage for,
111–13
USA Today, 35, 39, 47, 53

Veterans Administration, 137, 204
vision care, 165
discount clubs and, 114

wages, decline in real, 177–78
waiting period for elective procedures, 14,
25–26
Walgreens, 125–28
Wall Street Journal, 68, 73, 88, 122, 128,
129, 151
Wal-Mart, 81, 125–28
weight-loss programs, 78
Witt, Jim, 119–22
worksheets
flexible savings accounts, 194–95
health care and insurer log, 200
health plan selection, 196–97
prescription drug, 198–99
World Health Organization, 4
Wyss, Stephen L., 21–22, 27, 97, 109, 207

young adults
health savings accounts for, 82–83
university students, 111–13

about the author

FRED BROCK, a former business editor and current contributor to *The New York Times*, is the author of *Retire on Less Than You Think* and *Live Well on Less Than You Think*. He holds the R. M. Seaton Professional Journalism chair at Kansas State University. He has also been an editor and reporter covering politics, business, and finance for *The Wall Street Journal*, the *Houston Chronicle*, and the *Louisville Courier-Journal*. He lives in Manhattan, Kansas.

**You Can Have a Better Lifestyle Without a Bigger Paycheck
Learn How in These No-nonsense Guides from Fred Brock**
Available in paperback from Times Books

Retire on Less Than You Think

In this indispensable guide, *New York Times* columnist Fred Brock cuts through the mutual-fund industry hype and Social Security scares to deliver frank and pragmatic advice on retirement planning. The book offers the latest thinking on all the essentials for a smart and secure retirement, from finding untapped asset streams to building a reasonable budget based on your new lifestyle. It also includes a substantial list of national, regional, and online resources.

Live Well on Less Than You Think

Fred Brock challenges conventional financial wisdom again in this smart, down-to-earth primer on financial survival—and prosperity— in today's uncertain economy. Here Brock contests the hype that is driving money decisions during the working years—credit card debt, children's educational costs, stagnant wages—and shows readers how to analyze their true costs of living so that they can live debt- and worry-free, enjoying themselves and securing their future.

Health Care on Less Than You Think

Drawing on tested, popular strategies, Fred Brock tackles the most alarming financial issue facing Americans: the health-care crisis. In this one-stop guide to maximizing your coverage while minimizing your costs—with potential savings of thousands of dollars each year— he shows how to shop for coverage based on location, manage Medicare to protect your retirement, assess the value of health savings accounts, track down savings on prescription drugs, and more.

Learn more about these books by visiting www.henryholt.com.